365

QUICK & EASY TIPS

HOME CLEANING

QUICK & EASY TIPS
HOME CLEANING

Simple Techniques to Keep Your Home
Spotless and Polished Year Round

weldon**owen**

CONTENTS

▶ **GETTING STARTED CHECKLISTS**

KITCHEN

QUICK TIP: *Make a Better Fit*

QUICK TIP: *Line the Fridge*

QUICK TIP: *Wipe Up Spills Quickly*

QUICK TIP: *Out of Lemons?*

QUICK TIP: *Try a Tray*

QUICK TIP: *Sterilize Your Sponge*

► *KITCHEN CHECKLISTS*

BATHROOM

LAUNDRY

LIVING ROOM

DINING ROOM

BEDROOM

HOME OFFICE

CLEANING CHECKLISTS

CLEANING RECIPES

INDEX

CREDITS

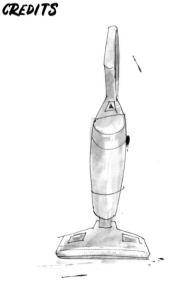

001 STOCK YOUR CADDY

Streamline housekeeping duties by assembling a cleaning caddy to contain all the necessary supplies needed to keep your home clean. A caddy eliminates time-draining, procrastinating searches for the right supplies and means fewer trips to the store or utility closet. Assemble supplies in a bucket or container with a handle and everything will be within arm's reach when you need it. Here's a checklist of suggestions for your essential caddy tools.

- Microfiber cloths
- Sponge
- Disposable wipes
- Duster
- Lint roller
- Toothbrush
- Scrub brush
- Grout brush
- Gloves
- Trash bags
- Cleaning solutions

QUICK TIP

SAVE TIME

Caddies make cleaning much quicker and efficient.

002 WIPE IT ALL UP

You'll want some options for wiping, dusting, and otherwise cleaning various surfaces.

MICROFIBER CLOTHS These soft, multipurpose cloths contribute to a healthier house. Woven from millions of very fine fibers, they snag dirt and bacteria in their web and sweep it away. Even dry or with a small amount of water, they are superior to paper towels or cotton rags when it comes to collecting dust and dirt. Because they absorb grime, clean them after each use by running them through the washing machine. Don't use fabric softener in the dryer with them—it clogs the fibers, reducing their ability to grab dirt.

THE CLASSIC SPONGE A sponge is an essential tool for absorbing spills and washing dishes or counters. Look for nonabrasive types that won't scratch the surface you're cleaning. After each use, clean and sanitize the sponge through a full cycle in the dishwasher or kill the germs in the microwave for two minutes. Be sure the sponge is wet.

DISPOSABLE WIPES Although reducing, reusing, and recycling as much as possible is the best approach, there are times when it's necessary to use disposable products like cleaning wipes. Pet accidents and on-the-go messes are great examples. Simply wipe up the mess with a disposable wipe and toss it in the trash.

A DUSTER Microfiber or feather dusters on an extension wand are invaluable in hard-to-reach spaces like ceiling fans, top shelves, corners, or under the bed.

A LINT BRUSH is a multipurpose tool that is often forgotten among all the cleaning supplies in the caddy. It removes lint from not only clothing but also handbag interiors, lampshades, curtains, furniture, car seats, and flooring. And if you have pets, it's great for animal fur.

003 HANG YOUR RUBBER GLOVES

Sticking your hands into damp rubber gloves is a repulsive feeling. Ensure they air out completely between uses by hanging them by the fingertips to dry. If you have space in the cabinet under your sink, mount a couple of clothespins to hold them. Another option is to hang them with clips onto a dedicated clothes hanger in your laundry room (above your utility sink is ideal for drips) when you're done cleaning.

004 DESIGNATE A DROP ZONE

If you share living space with roommates, get a basket to collect each person's random belongings. This way, if your friend's keys are on the counter when you're ready to cook, you know where to drop them. And it becomes a good first spot to look when something's missing. This system works well for kids, too!

005 KEEP TOWELS NEARBY

Stashing a spare roll of paper towels in every bathroom of your home is a smart strategy. Even if they're not your go-to for regular cleaning, they're perfect for sopping up drips or when your bathroom needs a quick wipedown, like when a friend stops by unexpectedly.

006 CLEAN YOUR AIR

If you suffer from allergies or are sensitive to odors, an air filter is an investment that can make your life a lot more comfortable and healthier. They come in different models to fit the size of your space and plug into a wall outlet. The best ones are quiet and unobtrusive in design. Say goodbye to irritating pollen, dust, smoke, cooking smells, and stagnant air.

007 FOLLOW RECYCLING RULES

Recycling guidelines can vary from place to place. If there are instructions on your recycling bin, do your best to follow them. Some common no-no's are:

- Food
- Liquid
- Straws
- Prescription bottles
- Cardboard pizza boxes
- Plastic bags
- Plastic cups and dishes

008
KNOW THE RULES FOR GLASS

Some communities are no longer accepting glass recycling, but if glass is allowed, make sure you always remove the lids from your glass bottles before recycling. If recycling glass isn't an option, then reuse your glass bottles and jars as vases, food storage containers, or drinking glasses. You can even buy squirt nozzles and pump lids to turn them into soap dispensers or spray bottles.

QUICK TIP

RESCUE A BROKEN MIRROR

Shattered mirror? Broken glass can't be recycled, but the frame can be salvaged. Use a staple gun to attach rows of twine or ribbon to the back of the mirror. Then use miniclothespins to display photos, notes, cards, or artwork.

009
AVOID THE LANDFILL

Construction debris is a major contributor to waste, but if you're planning on any demos or home renovations, you can recycle a lot of what's left behind. Pipes and metal junk can be taken to a metal recycling drop-off center, where they'll often pay cash for your donation. Salvage shops, such as the Habitat for Humanity ReStores, are happy to accept items that are in good condition but just not your style anymore, such as kitchen cabinets and bathroom fixtures.

010   BRUSH IT OFF

Great brushes for cleaning are toothbrushes, scrub brushes, grout brushes, and drinking-straw cleaning brushes. Each has its unique properties, so use them all accordingly.

TOOTHBRUSH A handy implement for dirty surfaces in the bathroom and kitchen, a toothbrush allows you to scrub messes and stains on a small scale.

SCRUB BRUSH A natural wooden bristle brush is a tried-and-true tool that cleans just about everything from pots and pans to outdoor furniture. When it's time to clean a wooden brush, douse it in warm, soapy water and remove stubborn dirt with an old toothbrush. Air-dry it with bristles facing down so water will drain from the wood and minimize the chances that it will warp or grow mildew.

GROUT BRUSH For those hard-to-clean stains, a brush that's designed specifically for grout is needed to lift dirt and grime. A grout brush is equipped with particularly stiff V-shaped bristles that can get into the grout lines easier and does an overall better job than other types of brushes.

DRINKING-STRAW CLEANING BRUSHES If you ordered a multipack of drinking-straw cleaning brushes for your water bottles and are wondering what to do with the extras, toss a couple in your cleaning kit. Their long shape, flexible handles, and stiff bristles are handy for cleaning tight spots and small pipes.

011 USE UP YOUR STASH

Looking for a purpose for all those plastic bags you collected from grocery delivery and pickup? They're just right for lining bathroom or home office trash cans. Add them to your caddy or stuff them into a cardboard paper-towel tube (easy to store in a vanity or desk drawer) and pull them out when you need them.

NOTE ABOUT SANITIZING GERMS

Remember that while natural cleaners can be useful for cleaning and getting that sparkle and shine, they don't quite cut it for sanitizing germy surfaces. For that, turn to an all-purpose cleaner. There are several plant-based disinfectants that are effective at killing bacteria and viruses.

012 RAID YOUR PANTRY

All-natural, homemade cleaning products work wonderfully and smell great. Best of all, they are safe for kids, the home, and the environment. Avoid relying on toxic, potentially harmful chemical solutions and turn to your pantry instead. It is a trove of environmentally friendly ingredients to be used as a foundation for homemade cleaning solutions.

BAKING SODA This natural ingredient is a cleaning and deodorizing workhorse, especially effective in eliminating offensive smells. It's also a mild abrasive.

DISTILLED WHITE VINEGAR Despite its strong scent, vinegar reigns supreme as an excellent cleaner. Add a couple drops of essential oil (lemon and clove are a nice combination) to tone down the smell.

LEMON JUICE Add this miracle ingredient to homemade recipes to eliminate odors, remove stains, freshen, and deodorize.

SALT An inexpensive pantry staple, salt can be used to clean many things in the home. Add 1/4 c. salt and hot water to burnt pans, let them soak, and then scour away!

LIQUID CASTILE SOAP This great multipurpose cleaner, originally made centuries ago in the Castile region of Spain, uses olive oil as its base and is still considered one of the best and most popular natural cleaners today.

MAKE IT YOURSELF

The ingredients listed in tips 012 and 014 (and a few more handy items) can be combined in a number of ways to make everything from furniture polish to glass cleaner to disinfectant, and more. These common household items are also inexpensive and often sold in bulk, so you can save money and extra trips to the store by combining them to make your own cleaners. All-natural recipes are included in the chapter in which they are used, as well as in the Cleaning Recipes section at the back of the book.

014 CREATE DIY CLEANERS

Common pantry items can be combined into natural, nontoxic cleaners that can be used throughout the house. Take the time to create your own products with these recipes and you'll be ready for everyday spills. Remember that while natural cleaners can be useful for cleaning and getting that sparkle and shine, they don't quite cut it for sanitizing germy surfaces. For that, turn to an all-purpose cleaner. There are several plant-based disinfectants that are effective at killing bacteria and viruses.

ALL-PURPOSE CLEANER

2 tsp. borax

$1/4$ tsp. liquid castile soap

10 drops lemon essential oil

Mix all ingredients with hot water in a 16-oz. spray bottle.

ALL-PURPOSE FLOOR CLEANER

1 tsp. almond castile soap

$1/4$ c. distilled white vinegar

10 drops orange essential oil

10 drops clove essential oil

Mix all ingredients with hot water in a 24-oz. spray bottle.

DISINFECTANT

2 tbsp. liquid castile soap

20 drops tea tree oil

Mix the soap and essential oil with hot water in a 16-oz. spray bottle.

NONABRASIVE VINEGAR CLEANER

1 part distilled white vinegar

2 parts water

5 drops essential oil

Combine the vinegar and water in a 16-oz. spray bottle. Add 5 drops of essential oil, such as lavender, grapefruit, orange, lemon, or peppermint, if you don't like the smell of vinegar.

GLASS CLEANER

$1/4$ c. distilled white vinegar

5 drops lemon essential oil

Mix all ingredients with hot water in a 16-oz. spray bottle.

015 AGREE ON RULES

When sharing spaces, come to a consensus on basic house policies about when and how little things get done. Staying on top of the small stuff, such as always tossing the old coffee pod from the Keurig, will keep cleaning tasks and clutter (and resentment!) from growing into bigger problems.

016 SET A TIMER

If it's a challenge to stick to a cleaning schedule, or you start to feel like you're the only one cleaning and no one else is pulling their weight, switch up your rhythm. Pick a few times when everyone is home and set a timer to get done as much as possible. Whenever you and your roommate are both home, maybe you each work on whatever's nagging you the most. Or you set a 15-minute timer before bedtime, and the whole family tackles the playroom. Small bursts of concentrated energy, especially when everyone is working together, add up.

017 IMPROVE YOUR WINDOWS

When was the last time you gave your windows any attention? Last week? Last month? Last year? Your windows need cleaning twice a year. A plan and the right tools will prevent it from being an overwhelming job. Washing the outside may work best as a weekend project, but you can divide the inside by room or a goal-oriented number of windows for each session. Chances are that when you finally get started, you'll wind up cleaning more than your goal. For best results, plan to clean while the sun is not directly shining on the glass since heat can dry the solution quickly, causing streaks. Here's how to do it right.

STEP ONE Spray the Glass Cleaner (see tip 014) on the glass. Vinegar breaks down the dingy film that may have built up on the panes, minimizing streaks.

STEP TWO Moving from top to bottom, wipe with a dry microfiber cloth. (It is important that the cloth is lint free, which all microfiber cloths are.) On inside windows that are not especially dirty, microfiber cloths make quick work of wiping away dirt and drying the glass.

STEP THREE To squeegee or not? Professional window cleaners swear by a squeegee as the fastest and most practical method, particularly for outside windows that take on more grime. Think of how well they work to clean your car windshield! On smaller divided-light windows, pull down from top to bottom. On larger sheets of glass, use horizontal swipes starting at the top. After each run, brush the squeegee with a rag to wipe away the dirt and water. Finish with the microfiber cloth, using your index finger tucked into a dry spot to go over edges and corners.

018

WIPE DOWN WINDOWS AND MIRRORS

Spray windows and mirrors with the Glass Cleaner (see tip 014) and wipe clean with a lint-free microfiber cloth. Avoid using newspaper as a cleaning tool. This advice worked once upon a time, and you'll still see it in some classic cleaning guides, but modern paper and dyes tend to leave smudgy streaks that require extra work to eliminate.

019

FRESHEN UP WINDOW COVERINGS

Over time, dust and dirt may creep their way into your window treatments without being immediately noticeable. To nip this problem in the bud, make it part of your routine to regularly vacuum window treatments inside and out with a dust-brush attachment, and spot-clean as needed. Once or twice a year (depending on the dust level), take them down, bring them outside, and shake them thoroughly. Wash or professionally clean window coverings as needed.

QUICK TIP

REUSE COTTON FABRIC AS RAGS

If you don't want to buy microfiber cleaning cloths, you can still get a streak-free shine on glass and mirrors with a scrap of 100-percent cotton. Old bedsheets and T-shirts work well. Just make sure they don't have any holes or screen-printed designs on them (you want them as uniform as possible). Cut the fabric into squares a bit bigger than you think you need, as the edges can curl or unravel with time.

020 CLEAN BLINDS AND SHUTTERS

Since tending to them can typically add a lot more time to your cleaning routines, blinds and shutters get overlooked more often than not. Be sure to give them the attention they need whenever you clean, and get into the habit of properly cleaning them monthly.

SPOT-CLEAN Using the All-Purpose Cleaner (see tip 014) and a microfiber cloth or a specialty tool designed to clean blinds and shutters, wipe away dirt as needed.

DUST MONTHLY Using a vacuum dust-brush attachment on the lowest setting, suction the dirt away. Glide the brush attachment horizontally (not vertically) along the blinds or shutters. Start at the top and move your way down, then reverse the blades and dust on the other side.

DEEP CLEAN If the dust has turned to gunk on removable blinds (as often happens in the kitchen, where steam and grease are in the air), it's time for a more thorough cleaning. Pull the blinds up all the way before lifting them off their supports for easier transport. Using a soft sponge, briefly soak and wash them in the bathtub to remove grime. Rinse well, then lay them out on towels to completely dry before rehanging them.

STAY ON THE SHADY SIDE

Whether your home has honey-comb, roman, balloon, or roller shades, they need to be cleaned regularly. And it's simpler than you might think! Keep the dust at bay and regularly attend to them to avoid the need for more intense cleaning later.

DUST Completely lower the shades and dust from top to bottom on both sides using the dust-brush attachment with the vacuum's suction on its lowest level. Covering the attachment with a thin fabric, such as cheesecloth or hosiery, will keep the suction from grabbing the fabric.

SPOT-CLEAN If you need to spot-clean fabric shades, test an area in a lower fold that doesn't show when the shades are partially pulled up. Dampen the area (do not saturate) and gently scrub with a solution of dish soap and water. Use a wet cloth to remove soap residue.

AIR OUT Consider occasionally taking shades down to hang on a line outside for a fresh breath of air.

DRY-CLEAN Delicate fabrics, such as silk and wool, need to go to a dry cleaner for a professional cleaning.

DEAL WITH DRAPERIES

Your vacuum's versatile dust-brush attachment isn't just for hard surfaces or blinds; it also works well on draperies. Here's a quick and easy way to keep those draperies fresh and clean with minimal effort.

STEP ONE Dust the top first. If there is a valance, pelmet, or cornice, be sure to first vacuum the top and sides, which are total dust magnets.

STEP TWO Whenever a vacuum is used to clean fabrics, it should be positioned on the lowest setting to prevent damage to the fabric.

STEP THREE Look down. Pay attention to where the curtain hits the floor; dust bunnies love to hide there and accumulate.

STEP FOUR Smell the fabric. Curtains absorb smells and smoke, so even if they appear clean, a more thorough cleaning may be in order.

023 REMEMBER DOORS AND BASEBOARDS

It's amazing how quickly your doors and baseboards collect dust. But once you add base-board maintenance to your routine, the process will go surprisingly fast. A duster or a small dust-brush attachment on a vacuum will make this task easier on your back. For resistant dirt, especially in the kitchen where grease settles, use the All-Purpose Cleaner (see tip 014) and scrub with a microfiber cloth. A toothbrush also helps for getting crud out of corners.

024

SWIPE THE SWITCH PLATES

Dirty fingers touch the switch plates several times a day. That alone should be enough to inspire you to regularly clean them. Slightly dampen a micro-fiber cloth with the All-Purpose Cleaner (see tip 014) and wipe away the grime. Disposable wipes will suffice when time is limited.

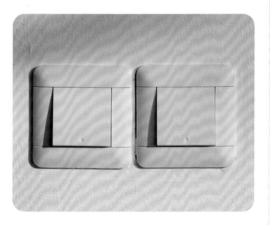

025 REMEMBER HOUSEHOLD ELECTRONICS

Oils, dirt, and germs tend to accumulate where we touch the most, so your Bluetooth speaker, remotes, and laptop are probably overdue for a wipe-down.

026 REACH FOR CEILINGS AND WALLS

Nab cobwebs weekly by using a duster with an extension wand. For a deeper cleaning, use your vacuum's dust-brush attachment, working from ceiling to floor so dust doesn't fall and cling to areas you've just cleaned. Though it may not be visibly apparent, the air circulation from HVAC units deposits fine dust all over walls. Wipe the walls at least once a year to get rid of this fine coating, or every season if your house is a dust magnet! And remember that not all walls are created equal. High-gloss enamel paint and washable wallpaper are a breeze to clean while latex paint and fine wallpaper beg for special care. The information in tips 027, 029, and 032 will help you sort through the right process for your particular walls.

027 KNOW YOUR PAINTS

The kind of paint, enamel or latex, will dictate its appropriate cleaning method. Enamel, or oil-based, paints stand up to daily wear and tougher cleaning than latex paints. That's why enamel paints are popular in kitchens, baths, and play areas. Both enamel and latex paints are available in a full range of finishes ranging from high-gloss, semigloss, satin, and eggshell to flat. Generally, the glossier the paint, the easier it is to wipe away dirt and remove crayon drawings. At the opposite end of the spectrum is a flat finish, which is easily marked and can tolerate only very limited cleaning methods. Eggshell and satin finishes gradually increase in glossiness, but are still delicate.

028

SAFELY DISPOSE OF PAINT

It's smart to store leftover paint for touch-ups in a cool, dark place such as your basement. You can even transfer it into a mason jar to save on space and make it a cinch to see what the colors are. When you don't need it anymore, search for a hazardous waste center in your area to drop off whatever remains. Habitat for Humanity will often accept donations as well. If it's latex paint, it can be mixed with kitty litter or sawdust. Once it's completely dry, you can put it out with your regular garbage for pickup.

QUICK TIP

STEAM CLEAN IN BETWEEN

For a quick refresh between deep cleanings, steaming your curtains is an easy task that makes a big impact. Not only does steam smooth out wrinkles that build up over time, but it can also blast away germs, odors, and dust. Travel garment steamers are effective, affordable, simple to use, and easy to store.

KEEP FINE
WALLPAPER BEAUTIFUL

To protect the color and pattern you love, regular vacuuming with a soft dust brush is the safest way to keep the paper clean. Save the water for smudges and noticeable dirt. Wetting wallpaper with water or cleaning solution can degrade the paper and weaken the adhesive. Scrubbing will remove the paper along with the stain! The golden rule for cleaning wallpaper is to use only a little moisture and light pressure. Use the following process for treating stains:

HOLD THE WATER Before applying any water, first test a small area in an inconspicuous place and leave it overnight to see if it dries without discoloring the paper or leaving a water spot. If water does not harm the paper, start with a barely damp sponge and gently wipe the soiled area to remove the dirt. Try a mildly soapy water solution if needed. Wipe it over the stain and let it dry before you wipe it again. This may seem tedious, but a slow process guards against fading or tearing wet paper.

APPLY CAREFULLY A thick paste of baking soda and water (as little water as needed to make a paste) is the last resort, but can be effective if used carefully. Smear it over the stain and let it rest for a few minutes. Stand by with a dry cloth beneath the paste so you can catch any water before it drips down the wall, then softly wipe the paste off with a damp cloth. You may need to repeat it several times; just make sure the wallpaper never gets too saturated.

ASK GRANDMA One cleaning method for wallpaper stains is an old household trick your grandmother may have used. Roll a slice of white or rye bread into a ball and use it as a natural eraser to remove stains. Dab it on the stain; don't rub. The gluten in the bread absorbs dirt and stains.

030 RESTORE WOOD PANELING

Most wood paneling has a factory coating to protect it, but it still will need regular dusting with a vacuum, feather duster, or microfiber cloth. Wood in family rooms where there's a lot of activity and a fireplace will call for a more intensive seasonal cleaning. Use this process for sealed wood paneling.

STEP ONE Add 1 tsp. mild dishwashing detergent to 24 oz. warm water in a spray bottle. Spray on walls, wiping with a slightly damp microfiber cloth as you go.

STEP TWO Mix $\frac{1}{2}$ c. vinegar in 1 gallon warm water. Wet a microfiber cloth in the solution, wringing out as much water as possible. Wipe the paneling to remove any soap residue.

STEP THREE Dry walls with a clean microfiber cloth.

STEP FOUR Polish by putting a small amount of jojoba oil on a microfiber cloth and buff to a shine.

031 HANDLE WITH CARE

Don't use water on unfinished wood walls! They should be dusted and vacuumed regularly to keep dirt from building up. Waxed or oiled woods will require special care. Regular dusting with a vacuum attachment or a microfiber cloth is essential. Periodically wipe them down with a soft cloth dipped in warm water and wrung almost dry. Change the cloth often and work right behind yourself to immediately dry the wood with a towel. Reapply the same type of wax or oil after cleaning.

032 SPOT-CLEAN WALLS

Walls, children, crayons, and markers seem to have a special relationship that can try your patience, even if it is momentarily charming. Walls attract all sorts of other stains such as grease, scuffs, soot, food, mold, and mildew. Here are reliable methods for getting rid of them and restoring your walls to their previous pristine appearance. Refer to the chart for targeted cleaning solutions, but be sure to test in an inconspicuous spot first!

STAIN	SURFACE	WHAT TO DO
CRAYON	Painted wall*	Dab white paste toothpaste (no gels) on the stain. Let it rest for a few minutes. Rinse off with a damp microfiber cloth. Dry.
	Nonwashable wallpaper	Use an art gum eraser to get rid of the stain.
PENCIL OR PEN	Painted wall*	Make a paste of baking soda and water. Rub the paste onto a microfiber cloth. Wipe stain. Rinse off. Remove paste completely. Dry.
	Nonwashable wallpaper	Use an art gum eraser to get rid of the stain.
BLACK MARKS	Painted wall*	Dab white paste toothpaste (no gels) on the stain. Let it rest for a few minutes. Rinse off with a damp microfiber cloth. Dry.
FINGERPRINTS	Washable or nonwashable wallpaper	Roll a piece of bread rolled into a ball, or an art gum eraser, over the mark.
GREASE SPOTS	Washable wallpaper	Mix talcum powder or cornstarch with a bit of water to make a paste on a microfiber cloth. Apply to stain. Let it rest for 10 minutes. Rinse with water (not too much). Dry.
	Nonwashable wallpaper	Hold a thick paper bag or layers of paper towels over the stain and briefly press with an iron on a low-heat setting. The grease should adhere to the paper.

*Works on glossy enamel paint, but test carefully before trying on any latex paint or on flat, eggshell, or satin enamel.

033 CARE FOR EXPOSED BRICK

It may not show dirt because of its rough surface and dark color, but exposed brick gets dirty just like any other wall. Brick is porous, so soot from a fireplace, as well as dirt and dust, find a welcome spot to roost. Regularly dust brick with a microfiber cloth or the dust-brush attachment on the vacuum cleaner.

STEP ONE Mix one part salt to one part mild dishwashing liquid or castile soap. Add just enough water to make a thick paste.

STEP TWO Apply the mixture to the wall, which may be easiest to do with your hands. Scrub the wall with a stiff scrub brush and leave the paste on for 10 minutes.

STEP THREE Remove the paste with a clean wet sponge. Rinse the sponge often in a bucket of clean water to remove any trace of the paste and its residue as you work. If the paste adheres to the brick, use a clean scrub brush to get it off.

034 CHALKBOARD WALLS BACK TO BLACK

To clean a chalkboard wall without damaging it, spray the All-Purpose Cleaner (see tip 014) onto a microfiber cloth, and then wipe down the wall from top to bottom. Frequently rinse the chalk dust off the cloth and repeat as necessary until your chalkboard wall is as fresh as when it was painted.

MAKE A GRAND ENTRANCE

Exterior doors must be seasonally cleaned. Outside doors take a beating—weather, dirty hands, spills, kicks, and more. It's going to happen. However, they are an introduction to your home, so you want doors to be as clean as possible. A door's materials govern your cleaning strategy, so use these tips for the most common door materials.

WOOD A solution of castile soap and water applied with a microfiber cloth will thoroughly clean the door and door surround. Start at the top, attacking tough stains, scuffs, or dirt with the cloth while being careful not to scratch paint or damage the decorative finish.

SLIDING GLASS Fingerprints and smudges stick out like a sore thumb on glass doors, but are easily eliminated with the Glass Cleaner (see tip 014). However, the slider tracks catch all sorts of crud, bugs, and spills that can eventually impede the mechanics of the doors. Use the vacuum's crevice attachment to dispose of dirt and debris in the track every time you vacuum the room's floor. A toothbrush may be needed to dislodge resistant gunk trapped in the tracks. The glass and metal frame should follow the window-cleaning schedule twice a year.

FIBERGLASS OR PAINTED STEEL Wipe clean with a soft cloth and mild, soapy water.

036 TIDY OUTDOORS

When the seasons change, your outdoor spaces require a little TLC. Sweep or power-wash dirt, cobwebs, and debris from your walkways, porches, decks, balconies, patios, and outdoor light fixtures. Wipe down your mailbox and exterior doors. Clean and/or store outdoor rugs, furniture, cushions, and umbrellas.

037 DON'T FORGET THE TRASH CAN

No matter how meticulous you are about using trash bags, things of unknown origin will make it to the bottom of trash cans. The key is to regularly clean them before the grime builds up! Put on gloves and take the can outside or put it in the shower. Thoroughly rinse it with hot, soapy water and use a scrub brush to dislodge stubborn gunk. Rinse and let it dry. Air-drying in the sun naturally disinfects, but spraying with the Disinfectant (see tip 014) is still recommended.

Doorknobs transfer germs and bacteria from person to person. Add cleaning them to your monthly chore list to keep knobs sparkling clean. To help eliminate the spread of illness, disinfect weekly during winter months, when colds and viruses run rampant. Spray a microfiber cloth with the Disinfectant (see tip 014) and then thoroughly scrub each doorknob in your house.

OLD COPPER, BRASS, AND BRONZE These knobs tend to tarnish over time, so special care is needed if you want them to look new again. However, if you're a preservationist or nostalgist, you may prefer the tarnished look. In any case, regularly clean them to remove dirt and grime. To clean, dampen a cloth with the Disinfectant and thoroughly wipe the knob. Dry and buff with a second microfiber cloth, taking care not to leave any moisture or disinfectant behind.

To polish copper and brass, mix 2 tbsp. salt with just enough lemon juice to make a thick paste. Rub it on and let stand for 30 minutes. Wash off with a cloth dampened with soapy water, and rinse with a clean damp cloth and dry. For bronze, use 2 tbsp. baking soda with lemon juice to make a paste, and follow the same instructions.

NEW FINISHES New hardware is often treated with a lacquer finish to hold its high polish. Regularly clean it, but do not apply any polishing paste, or risk stripping off the protective lacquer (unless it begins to tarnish, which signals that it lacks a lacquer finish).

NICKEL, CHROME, STAINLESS STEEL, AND OIL-RUBBED BRONZE Knobs are available in an abundance of finishes, including options for polished or brushed (also called satin finish). The Disinfectant is a combination of all-natural products and should be safe for any of these finishes, but if in doubt, check with the manufacturer.

CRYSTAL AND GLASS Crystal is easy to care for. Carefully wash with warm, soapy water and a soft cloth and immediately dry with a cotton towel to prevent water spots.

039 START AT THE BOTTOM

Who doesn't love walking into a room with clean and shiny floors? Maintaining floors daily makes the entire house feel cleaner (even if it really isn't!). So take a few minutes every day and clean them. If you don't have time to deep clean, no problem. Quickly cover the high-traffic areas with your vacuum, as vacuuming picks up more dust and debris than sweeping or dust-mopping. Spot-clean messes before they harden with a damp microfiber cloth. A quick daily cleaning will remove dirt, twigs, small stones, and other hard debris that gets tracked inside and will scratch any floor if not quickly removed. This is your first line of defense.

MOVE FAST If spills are immediately addressed, there's less likelihood of tough spots. Wipe with a damp cloth and dry with another cloth. When tackling a particularly difficult stain, remember that the top priority is preventing floor damage.

WATCH THE WATER Too much water can damage almost all flooring materials. Be thorough, but use a light touch when it comes to liquids. Never mop without first sweeping or vacuuming to remove debris that will scratch with swipes of the mop.

LOSE THE SHOES Eliminate dirty floors at the source by implementing a "no shoes" rule. The primary reason floors get dirty is people wearing shoes in the house. If you have a medical issue and need to wear them, designate a clean pair that you can switch to when you get home, or wear slippers.

BREAK IT UP If it's daunting to tackle cleaning all your floors in one day, split up the tasks over a couple consecutive days. First vacuum, and then mop. Or divide floor cleaning by zones, such as main living area on one day and bedrooms on the next. Is it easier to do the bathroom floors when you clean the bathrooms? Figure out a system that works best for you.

040

USE A SPRAY MOP

Streamline floor cleaning by switching out your old-school, germ-filled mop and bucket of water with a spray mop. It saves a lot of time and money, and it's more sanitary. Look for a spray mop that allows you to mist a floor-cleaning solution onto the floor just ahead of the flathead microfiber pad. Microfiber pads can be laundered (without bleach or fabric softener), and even disposable refills can be washed several times before tossing. This application is not only easier, but is more sanitary than wringing out an old-fashioned cotton mop head. Also avoid mops or sweepers that require same-brand disposable sheets, which often have toxic chemicals.

QUICK TIP

AVOID COSTLY MISTAKES

Though cleaning practices for many flooring materials are similar, using the wrong technique or cleaner can be disastrous. Be sure that you know exactly which kind of flooring is installed in each room before doing any intensive cleaning. Some floors, such as hardwood, can take on a hazy or cloudy film if not treated properly, or even become warped if too much water is absorbed. Scrubbing your laminate, bamboo, or wood floors too firmly can scuff them or wear off the finish. Concrete and some stone and tile floors are porous and can absorb harsh cleansers, leading to permanent stains or color changes.

041

WASH TWICE

For the cleanest of clean floors (or if you've been falling down on the job for a little while), consider going over them twice in opposite directions.

CLEAN YOUR BROOM

Remember that it's useless to clean with a dirty tool. It doesn't take long for your broom's bristles to become matted with dust, dirt, and hair. Solve this problem by raking a wide-tooth comb through the bristles. Then fill your mop bucket with some warm water and a couple drops of dishwashing soap. Swish the broom around in the water, and then let it air-dry completely before sweeping again.

NOTE: Remember that while natural cleaners can be useful for cleaning and getting that sparkle and shine, they don't quite cut it for sanitizing germy surfaces. For that, turn to an all-purpose cleaner. There are several plant-based disinfectants that are effective at killing bacteria and viruses.

FIND THE RIGHT FLOOR SOLUTION

Opinions about what works best to clean floors differ, but homemade, natural cleaning solutions are popular options for many. They are healthier for the family, gentler on floors, inexpensive, and simply better for the environment. Here are several homemade spray-mop solutions that can be used throughout the home. Don't waste another cent buying premade, expensive floor cleaners! If you are unsure whether a cleaning solution is right for your floors, spot-test, or ask your flooring manufacturer. Feel free to swap in your favorite essential oils to create a personalized scent!

HARDWOOD FLOOR CLEANER

1 tsp. almond castile soap
10 drops lemon essential oil

Mix all ingredients with hot water in a 24-oz. spray bottle. Use sparingly to minimize the chance of warping; do not use on unsealed hardwoods.

TILE FLOOR CLEANER

$1/4$ c. distilled white vinegar
15 drops orange essential oil

Mix all ingredients with hot water in a 24-oz. spray bottle.

ALL-PURPOSE FLOOR CLEANER

1 tsp. almond castile soap
$1/4$ c. distilled white vinegar
10 drops orange essential oil
10 drops clove essential oil

Mix all ingredients with hot water in a 24-oz. spray bottle.

LAMINATE FLOOR CLEANER

$3/4$ c. distilled white vinegar
$3/4$ c. rubbing alcohol
10 drops peppermint essential oil
$3/4$ c. hot water

Mix all ingredients in a 24-oz. spray bottle. Use sparingly to minimize the chance of warping.

VINYL FLOOR CLEANER

$1/4$ c. distilled white vinegar
3 tbsp. borax
10 drops lemon essential oil
10 drops lavender essential oil

Mix all ingredients with hot water in a 24-oz. spray bottle.

HANDLE HARDWOOD

Most hardwood floors are sealed with a urethane finish, but not all. Sticklers for historic authenticity may prefer not to seal heart pine or other original wood that has developed a patina over time. A urethane coating on your hardwood floor extends the time between refinishings, but your diligence in cleaning will also be a factor. Polyurethane is essentially a plastic coat intended to maintain a comparatively care-free, long-term finish, and there's a long list of products that will etch and dull the finish. Never use an oil soap, acrylic "mop and shine" products, paste or liquid wax, vinegar, or ammonia, and avoid abrasive rubbing. Steam cleaning is not recommended, as it may damage the coating and the wood beneath.

DO IT DAILY For daily cleaning, use a microfiber dust mop or vacuum. A slightly damp mop is okay, if the floor is immediately dried.

CLEAN SEALED FLOORS To do a deeper clean of a sealed floor, fill a spray bottle with the Hardwood Floor Cleaner (see tip 042) and mist a 4′ × 4′ section. Mop back and forth along the grain of the wood (following the length of the boards) to minimize streaking, then continue to another section.

CARE FOR OILED WOOD Regular cleaning is even more important here because a penetrating oil finish protects wood from drying, but will allow stains to penetrate. Vacuum often and mop with clear water once a week. Avoid excess moisture when mopping, and do not steam clean this type of flooring. Never use ammonia, detergents, soaps, or commercial cleaners.

HOLD THE WATER ON WAX If your floors have a waxed finish instead of a polyurethane seal, vacuum them with the floor brush. Water will damage wax, so use a damp cloth to immediately wipe up spills.

USE A LIGHT TOUCH ON BAMBOO

Too much grit or too much water will damage this renewable, eco-friendly material. Bamboo is prone to scratching from everyday dirt that gets tracked into the house. Sweep daily, but use a soft-bristled broom or microfiber dust mop, or vacuum with the floor-brush attachment. Mop weekly with the Hardwood Floor Cleaner (see tip 042) by misting a small area and following with a microfiber mop. Don't let the cleaner pool on the floor. Avoid ammonia, vinegar, and other acidic cleaners.

045 KEEP LAMINATES LOVELY

Laminate floors are made from a remarkable likeness of wood flooring, encased in a plastic laminate to get the look of hardwood without the cost and care. However, laminate floors cannot be refinished, so it's especially important to take good care of them.

SPOT TREATMENT For daily cleaning, use a microfiber mop or vacuum. For more thorough cleaning, spray the Laminate Floor Cleaner (see tip 042) onto a mop and work in small sections. Immediately wash off with a damp mop, and thoroughly dry with a towel.

046 PAMPER STONE

Just as silk blouses need a little special handling, so do natural stone floors. Liquids can penetrate stone. A protective sealant, generally applied at installation, boosts stain resistance, but won't make a floor stainproof.

DAILY CARE Daily removal of dirt and grit is as critical for stone as it is for any floor. Ground underfoot by walking, tiny particles will scratch. A dry microfiber mop minimizes chances of scratching.

KEEP IT CLEAN Use a damp mop with clean water only, changing the water often. Dry the floor with a towel or a microfiber pad to prevent water spots. Seasonally and after a widespread spill, mop using the Tile Floor Cleaner (see tip 042), then rinse thoroughly with clean water before drying the floor.

FIGHT STAINING Quickly blot a liquid spill with a dry cloth to absorb as much as possible. Dampen a white cloth with a mild soap-and-water solution and briefly tamp the stain until it stops appearing on the cloth. Don't saturate the area. Rinse with clear water and dry with a cloth—even water leaves stains if left long enough. Wine, colas, and acidic foods react with stone—clean them up fast! Avoid abrasive brushes or sponges and ammonia-based cleaners.

047 CARE FOR CORK

A naturally sustainable and nontoxic material, cork is also resilient, making it easier on the feet and back than many other surfaces. It is quite porous, so all cork flooring must be sealed. The sealant applied to cork is a thin coat, and tiny particles that aren't visible will scratch it, so be meticulous in daily cleaning with a broom, microfiber dust mop, or vacuum floor-brush attachment.

MOP CLEAN Use a damp mop only with the All-Purpose Floor Cleaner (see tip 042). Avoid saturating with water. If cork hasn't air-dried by the time you finish mopping, dry it with a clean towel. Never use any commercial product on cork, nor abrasive sponges that can scratch right through the thin seal on top of the cork.

GET THE JUMP ON SPILLS Never give spills a chance to soak in—immediately wipe up as much as possible. Spray with the All-Purpose Floor Cleaner, rubbing gently with a microfiber cloth. Rinse with clean water and dry with a towel.

048

GET A
CONCRETE SOLUTION

Concrete, long used as an industrial floor-ing, has recently become popular inside the house as well. Naturally porous, it should be sealed for easy maintenance—although the sealant only makes it stain resistant, not stainproof. It is possible to seal an existing concrete floor, but it's a job best left to professionals. Daily clean-ing doesn't require anything special beyond the basics.

SOAP AND RINSE Never use ammonia or vinegar on concrete, as they can dam-age the sealant. To make a natural cleaning solution for concrete, mix 1 tsp. of mild soap (such as citrus castile soap) into 1 gal. of warm water. Work in small sections with a damp mop, frequently dipping the mop and wringing out as much soapy water as possible. Then make another run over the floor, using clean water to remove soap residue.

TREAT SPILLS Any substance that might stain cannot be allowed to sit. Immedi-ately clean spills with a castile soap solu-tion. If the stain is still apparent, leave the solution on for 20 minutes and scrub with a stiff-bristled brush.

049 LOVE THAT LINOLEUM

Everything old is new again, and homeowners who might once have ripped out linoleum floors are finding a new appreciation for its retro-cool designs and easy care. Made from organic materials (primarily linseed oil, plus a number of additives such as cork, pine resin, and minerals), it is antibacterial and nonallergenic. Linoleum can be swept or vacuumed like most floors. For more thorough cleaning, use a spray mop that's been dampened with the All-Purpose Floor Cleaner (see tip 042) or spray a small section of the floor at a time, just big enough that you can mop it right away. Treat tougher spots by dampening a cloth with the All-Purpose Floor Cleaner and gently rubbing the mark. Never use strong alkaline cleaners such as ammonia, bleach, or hydrogen peroxide.

TREAT TILES RIGHT

As with wood floors, tiles also come in a wide range of materials and finishes. Whether they're made of ceramic or porcelain, flooring tiles can be either glazed or polished, or unglazed. Daily care is the same for all these surfaces, but use the right techniques for anything beyond the basics (by which we mean sweeping, cleaning with a microfiber dust mop, or using the floor-brush attachment for your vacuum). Tile is almost always grouted; for grout-cleaning techniques, see tip 010.

CERAMIC OR PORCELAIN TILES	TO WASH	SPOT TREATMENT	BE CAREFUL
GLAZED OR POLISHED	Damp-mop with the Tile Floor Cleaner (see tip 042) and dry it using a second microfiber cloth or another mop to avoid leaving any water spots and streaking.	Opt for a soft-bristled toothbrush to avoid scratching the finish. Use a small amount of the Tile Floor Cleaner on tough stains, but immediately remove the cleaner with a damp cloth or a mop and hot water.	This is no place for scrub brushes and stiff bristles, as they will scratch the polished finish. Ammonia and bleach are no-no's that can discolor the tile and grout.
UNGLAZED	Saturate a small area, 3 or 4 feet, with the Tile Floor Cleaner and, after a few minutes, wipe away. Then follow up with a clean, dry microfiber cloth to remove moisture, working in manageable sections.	Unglazed tiles are very porous, so any stain must immediately be cleaned before it can sink into the tile. Scrape or wipe up at once, and if needed, scrub the area with a toothbrush.	Don't let water or other liquids sit on the surface. Water stains can easily develop, and the unglazed tile can become a home for mold or mildew.

051 MAINTAIN A VINYL FLOOR

Soft underfoot and easy to maintain, vinyl comes in sheet form and tiles. The tiles may imitate ceramic tiles, natural stone, or wood. Quality, or grading, considerably varies. What does not vary is how simple, regular cleaning is essential to prolonging the floor's life. Nothing fancy is necessary for daily cleaning, just the basic broom, microfiber dust mop, or proper vacuum cleaner attachment.

MOP IT UP Dampen a mop with clean water and spray with the Vinyl Floor Cleaner (see tip 042). The vinegar will cut through grease and disinfect while the essential oils will restore shine.

TREAT SCUFFS Vinyl will scuff, but gently rubbing with a bit of liquid wax like jojoba will remove scuffs. Then apply the Vinyl Floor Cleaner to remove the oil. Spot-clean food stains with a toothbrush and a paste of baking soda and water, rinsing well with clean water.

PROLONG THE FLOOR'S LIFE
Abrasive cleaners and applicators will scratch vinyl, and soap, detergents, and acrylic "mop and shine" products will dull the finish. Ammonia will likely cause cracks in the surface, and paste waxes or solvent-based polishes can damage the material.

CHECK YOUR CARPETS AND RUGS

Before you put any cleaner on a rug or carpet, find out what kind of fiber it's made of: wool, silk, cotton, another natural fiber, or synthetic. Cleaning techniques and stain removal guidelines differ. It's always a good idea to consult the owner's manual or manufacturer's website if you have any questions, but here are some basics on the most common materials.

WOOL Perhaps the most durable and resilient of fibers, wool nevertheless has a few specific quirks. When vacuuming, make certain the beater bar—the spinning bar under the vacuum attachment that lifts dirt and hair off the ground—is set on "high" so that it barely brushes against the top of the fibers. Overly aggressive beating can lead to pilling when it comes to wool. Instead of instinctively paralleling the edge of the rug with the vacuum, try a V-shaped trajectory that prevents crushing the fibers. Also, go slowly to give the vacuum enough time to suck up all the dust.

SILK Both silk rugs and silk patterns woven within a wool rug will require caution when cleaning. Treat stains with lukewarm water only. Try using the upholstery-brush attachment instead of the beater bar, which can change the texture of a silk rug.

PLANT FIBERS Plant-based natural fiber rugs, such as sisal, seagrass, jute, and hemp, are favorites for their natural texture and casual good looks. With the exception of seagrass, which is water resistant and therefore more stain resistant, natural-fiber rugs will readily absorb water and stains. Blot—don't rub—any spill with a microfiber cloth or clean white towel. Even water, if not removed immediately, can mix with the dirt in a rug and create a dark stain. Scrape up any solid substance with a spoon and let the rest dry. Gently brush and vacuum to remove the rest.

Natural fibers need more frequent vacuuming than most rugs, as dirt will cut into the fibers when ground in by foot traffic. Instead of the beater bar on your vacuum, consider using an upholstery-brush or dust-brush attachment. Both are softer and better suited to getting between tight weaves. Move the vacuum back and forth along the length of the rug and then vacuum again from side to side. Working in both directions picks up dirt trapped in the weave.

SYNTHETICS Artificially made, synthetic fibers are inherently stain resistant. Though you still need to quickly respond to stains, you'll find them much easier to remove in comparison to natural fibers.

053 PRESERVE AN ANTIQUE RUG

Antique rugs have held up to decades, if not centuries, of wear. With proper care, you can keep your antique rug in great condition for the next generation.

SHAKE IT OFF Shake out the rug if it's small enough. Carpets absorb odors and dust. It's a good idea to expose the rug to air at least once a year, but avoid putting it in direct sunlight. Rotate the rug once or twice during the year to evenly distribute wear from too much traffic.

VACUUM CAREFULLY Always vacuum on the lowest suction setting. Stay away from the fringe; you risk damaging it if it gets sucked into the attachment. If a lower setting is not an option, sweep with a broom. With either method, turn the rug over and clean both the front and back.

054 SIZE UP AN AREA RUG

The rug world has exploded with all manner of graphic, modern, and traditional designs. With so many handsome possibilities available, design leaders will now often layer area rugs on top of larger carpets. Take care of your smaller rugs and they'll eventually become beautiful vintage treasures.

KEEP IT CLEAN Vacuum both the front and back of the rug as well as the floor or carpet underneath. If possible, shake the rug outside to dislodge resistant dirt.

055 GO WASHABLE

Machine-washable rugs are a lifesaver for those with kids and pets. If messes are frequent in your home, it may be worth exploring this route. Another idea is to consider opting for an indoor/outdoor rug (made of polypropylene) for high-traffic areas or under dining tables. They are super durable and can literally be power-washed when they need a deep clean!

056 CARE FOR COWHIDE

Cowhide rugs have really caught on, in part because of their easy maintenance. Vacuum in the direction that the hair falls, using an upholstery-brush attachment rather than a beater bar. Move quickly to clean up spills with warm, soapy water, but don't saturate the hide.

057 SAVE THE SHEEPSKIN

Be gentle when washing a sheepskin rug, cleaning it in a way that is safe for both the leather pelt and the long, luxurious sheepskin fibers. If you don't specifically know that you can machine-wash your sheepskin rug, hand-wash it in a sink or bathtub.

Brush the rug using a sheepskin carding brush—a tool with long metal bristles—and then shake the rug out to remove as much dirt as possible before washing it in cold water with a mild liquid detergent. Do not use wool washes or laundry detergents, particularly ones that include enzymes or bleach. Swish the rug gently in the water without scrubbing to avoid matting.

Drain and refill the sink or tub as often as is needed until the water is running clear. Dry the rug flat afterward, away from direct sunlight and heat; resist trying to hurry the drying process so as not to harm the rug. Once the rug is fully dried, brush it again with the carding brush.

058 WASH FLOOR VENTS

Twice a year, or whenever they're looking cruddy, give your floor vents a good cleaning. They pop right up, and metal ones can go in the dishwasher. Do your whole house's worth in one load. Wipe down wood floor vents with a cleaning cloth and warm, soapy water and then let them air-dry on a towel.

059 STAY ON TOP OF CARPETS

With wall-to-wall carpet (as well as a large area rug or a throw rug), regular vacuuming is essential to keeping a clean house. Carpets will look fresh and clean, and they'll also last longer. Dirt and grit builds up in carpets and can fray the fibers.

Most carpets need cleaning only once a week, but high-traffic areas, such as the foyer and main living spaces, need it more frequently. And while you're at it, shake out smaller rugs. By staying on top of a weekly routine, you only need to shampoo carpets once a year.

060 CARE FOR YOUR VAC

If your vacuum won't spin or doesn't seem to be picking up everything it should, check your brush. If it's full of hair, you'll need to cut it out using a pair of scissors. Vacuum canisters, brushes, filters, removable hoses, and nozzles can be rinsed well with hot water (do it in a sink or tub).

061

LIFT STAINS NATURALLY

Sometimes, a stain needs just a little help to come out, and a little bit of soap and water can lift it right out. For tougher stains, white vinegar will provide a boost that breaks up the staining culprit.

VINEGAR-BASED CARPET STAIN REMOVER

1 tbsp. castile soap
1 tbsp. white vinegar
2 c. warm water

Mix all ingredients in a 16-oz. spray bottle.

BASIC CARPET STAIN REMOVER

$1/4$ tsp. castile soap

Mix soap with water in a 16-oz. spray bottle.

062 ACT IMMEDIATELY

The inevitable misfortune of a spill or tracked mud is bound to happen. Spot-treating carpet stains requires patience and tenacity. It may take repeated treatments to completely clean a stain, but the basic process is always the same.

BLOT THE STAIN Act immediately to absorb as much as possible or scrape up thicker spills with a spoon.

SPRAY IT ONCE Directly apply the appropriate stain remover (see tip 061) onto the stain. Be stingy with the amount of solution and water you put on the carpet, though—if the backing gets saturated, it's prone to mildew.

RESIST RUBBING Horizontal motions will only spread the stain. Instead, blot the stain with a damp cloth, moving from the outside of the stain toward the center.

TEST AND REPEAT With a clean spot on the cloth, check to see if the stain transfers to the cloth. If it does or if you can still see the stain on the carpet, repeat spraying and blotting until the stain is gone.

RINSE LIGHTLY Always end with a cold-water rinse, spraying the treated spot with clean water and blotting as needed to completely remove all the cleaning solution.

DRY IT OUT Remove as much moisture as possible with a dry, clean cloth.

063 FIGHT COMMON STAINS NATURALLY

A clean white cotton cloth is the best tool for the common stains below. Use white, as colors might react with your cleaning solvent and bleed into the carpet's fibers. Cotton cloths are the most absorbent, more environmentally friendly, and will not degrade with use. See tip 061 for the stain remover recipes.

IDENTIFY THE STAIN	TREAT IT WELL
Tomato-Based Sauces (e.g., Spaghetti Sauce, Ketchup, Barbecue Sauce)	Start with the Basic Carpet Stain Remover. If the stain is still there, step up to the Vinegar-Based Carpet Stain Remover. Rinse.
Wine, Juice, Berries, Chocolate, Sodas	Apply the Vinegar-Based Carpet Stain Remover and repeat as necessary. Rinse.
Coffee, Tea	Apply the Vinegar-Based Carpet Stain Remover and repeat as necessary. Rinse.
Oil-Based Food (e.g., Salad Dressings, Butter, Olive Oil)	Immediately sprinkle with baking soda and leave it for 10 minutes to absorb the oil. Vacuum lightly, then apply the Vinegar-Based Carpet Stain Remover as needed. Rinse.
Milk Products	Use a spoon and cloth to remove the spill from the carpet. Spray with the Basic Carpet Stain Remover. To eliminate a lingering spoiled-dairy smell, sprinkle with baking soda and allow it to sit overnight. Loosen with a dull knife in the morning and vacuum.
Dirt, Soil, Mud	Use a spoon or soft brush to remove as much as possible. Apply the Vinegar-Based Carpet Stain Remover and repeat as needed. Rinse.
Red Clay	Brush away as much as possible with a toothbrush. Put $\frac{1}{4}$ c. salt in a bowl and add just enough white vinegar to make a paste. Put the paste on the stain and leave for several hours. Rinse, let dry, and vacuum.
Urine	Use successive dry cloths to absorb as much liquid as possible. Mix equal parts white vinegar and water and spray on the carpet. Blot with a white cotton cloth, changing cloths often, and continue until all color is gone. If the stain or odor persists, generously sprinkle baking soda, leave it overnight, then vacuum.
Feces, Vomit	With gloves, use a spoon or spatula to remove as much as you can from the carpet. Blot any liquid, and apply the Vinegar-Based Stain Remover as needed. Sprinkle baking soda on the spot and let rest for 15 minutes. Vacuum.

064 LIGHT THE WAY

Lighting can change the mood of a room with a flip of a switch, so it's easy to take it for granted—until a bulb burns out or the lamplight dims because the shade is so dusty. Lamps need to be part of your weekly cleaning routine, while other fixtures need attention every six months to a year. When done weekly, lamps take only minutes to clean. Put it off and the job becomes more complicated. Gently wiping bulbs with a microfiber cloth greatly increases the amount of light emitted, particularly if you've never done it before.

065 BRIGHTEN LAMPSHADES

A quick, light weekly cleaning is essential for preserving your lampshades. By the time you notice a layer of dust or dirt on the lampshade, the only resort may be to toss the shade and buy another. Dust that settles on a shade turns to grime from moisture in the air, discoloring the shade. Heat from the lightbulb accelerates the darkening of a stain on the shade. Devote a few seconds to cleaning your lampshades and enjoy them for a long time.

DUST Dusting is critical with paper shades because they cannot be washed without becoming stained, warped, or damaged. Other shade materials that are attached to the frame with glue instead of stitching will also come apart in water, so keep up with the dusting.

Get into the habit of dusting the lamps and sconces (bulbs, base, and shade) every time you dust a room. Work when the light is off and cool to the touch. A microfiber cloth is best because it will pick up the dust instead of brushing it down onto the table or the floor.

VACUUM If you prefer, clean lampshades when you vacuum. Gently wipe the shade with the dust-brush attachment. Avoid suctioning directly on the fringe or other decorative trim; slide hosiery over the dust brush to keep from pulling off the trim.

TOOLS You can also use a clean paintbrush (1″–2″ wide) or a lint roller to remove dust from the shade. Find a method that is easy for you so you're more likely to do it.

WASH A FABRIC LAMPSHADE

Examine your shades before cleaning them because not all are washable. Fabric shades sewn onto a wire frame can and should be washed at least once a year. Sewn fabric shades, such as cotton, linen, and even silk, can be carefully washed by hand. Plastic shades can be sponged clean with water and mild soap, then completely dried.

It's tricky to spot-clean a fabric lampshade; rubbing one spot can damage the fabric and create a hole. Putting water or soap on one spot may simply replace a stain with a water spot. When you discover a stain, it's often best to clean the entire shade.

STEP ONE Dust first to remove as much dust and dirt as you can.

STEP TWO Fill a bathtub or a deep sink with enough lukewarm water to be able to immerse the shade. Add 1 tbsp. of castile soap. Don't use dishwashing soap or detergent!

STEP THREE Holding the shade by its wire frame, dip the shade and swirl it gently in the water until it appears clean. Drain the dirty water and refill the tub or sink with cool water. Continue to dip and gently swirl the shade until all soap and dirt is gone. Drain and refill until the water is running clear after rinsing the shade.

STEP FOUR Dry the shade away from direct sunlight. A hairdryer on a "cool" setting can speed the process; avoid the "hot" setting.

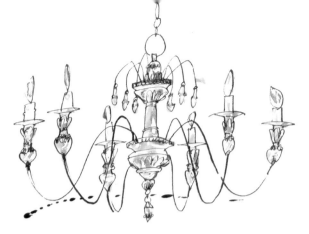

 SHINE GLASS SHADES

Sconces often have glass shades; wash these by hand in warm, soapy water once a year. Put towels in the sink to protect the shades, and don't use a dishwasher. Dry completely before returning them to the fixture.

Many pendant lights also have glass shades, especially in the kitchen. If they are not removable, you may need a ladder. Turn the electricity off at the panel. Then clean the shades with a sponge and soapy water from a bucket you can securely take up the ladder with you. Change the water often to remove built-up layers of dirt. Rinse the glass with a clean sponge and a bucket of clear water until the glass is shining.

068 REVIVE THE LAMP BASE

Lamps of all sorts as well as wall and ceiling fixtures can be made from a wide range of materials. Here's how to handle some of the most common ones you'll see.

MYSTERY METALS Many metal lighting fixtures are manufactured with various lacquered, painted, or powder-coated finishes, which can be potentially damaged by cleaning products and scrubbing. When buying a new fixture, ask at the time of purchase how to clean it. Otherwise, it's often a guessing game to identify the finish. If that's the case, wipe it off with clear water on a slightly damp cloth and then immediately dry the metal fixture.

BRASS AND COPPER If tarnish appears, your fixtures don't have a lacquered finish or the finish is breaking down and needs to be stripped. To polish tarnished brass and copper, sprinkle a generous amount of table salt on a lemon half and rub. Use as many lemons as needed to cover the surface. Wipe with a mild soap-and-water solution on a soft cloth. Dampen another cloth and rinse the soap off, then dry.

WOOD Dust unfinished wood. For stained or varnished woods, apply the Furniture Polish (see tip 267) with a soft cloth and buff with a clean cloth. Painted wood just needs a barely damp cloth and clear water; dry quickly with a soft cloth.

069 MAKE CHANDELIERS SPARKLE

Weekly dusting with a microfiber cloth is the best way to keep a chandelier looking good, but often, the fixture is not reachable. Opt for a microfiber duster on an extension wand for this delicate work. Once a year, plan on a serious cleaning, either by working on a ladder or by taking the fixture down from the ceiling to work on it. In either case, turn the electricity off at the panel.

SNAP A PICTURE If the chandelier has a complex design, take a few snapshots of it before you take the chandelier apart—you'll be glad you did when you have to find a piece that doesn't seem to go anywhere! Spread a drop cloth beneath the work area. Remove all breakable bulbs. Use protective eyewear if you're working from a ladder.

CLIMB A LADDER When cleaning a crystal or glass chandelier while you're on a ladder, spray the Glass Cleaner (see tip 014) onto a microfiber cloth and gently wipe the pieces. Never spray cleaner onto the fixture itself! Wipe each crystal and dry with a clean microfiber cloth.

TAKE IT DOWN If you're able to take a crystal or glass chandelier down from the ceiling, this complex project becomes a much easier job. Remove the crystals carefully, paying attention to how they are attached so you can correctly reassemble them when you're done.

070 LOOK UP

Flush-mounted lights need cleaning at least once a year. Remove all but the mounting hardware. Chandeliers require special work (see tip 069), but every fixture deserves attention.

CEILING FIXTURES Remove and clean all but the mounting hardware at least once a year. Wash glass by hand in mild, soapy water, rinse well, and dry before reattaching. Clean metal covers with soapy water, just using a sponge or cloth to apply the cleaner, rinse, and dry well before reattaching. If you find moths and insects on the glass fixture, consider taking the fixture down more often for cleaning.

DRUM SHADES Pendant lights with drum shades can be cleaned with the vacuum extension and the dust-brush attachment. If the shade is fabric, follow guidelines in tip 066.

071 CHOOSE WISELY

When choosing or replacing light fixtures, think about how the style will impact its ease of cleaning. Bowl pendant lights are notorious for collecting dust and bugs, while bell-shaped lighting is a breeze to dust from below.

CHECKLISTS

It might seem daunting at first glance, but don't be intimidated—this list is just meant to be a guide, a framework of suggestions. Tailor the to-do's to your life: whether or not you have pets, children, a housekeeper, or a need to keep things tidy or not. Make the list work for you according to your reality. Numbers refer to the general cleaning tips, so make sure to reference the appropriate supporting tips to address specific materials and circumstances.

DAILY
- ☐ Whole-house pickup
- ☐ Spot-clean spills and potential stains 002, 014
- ☐ Sweep or vacuum floors 039

WEEKLY
- ☐ Dust window treatments 019
- ☐ Dust doors and baseboards 023
- ☐ Clean switch plates 024
- ☐ Dust ceilings and walls 026
- ☐ Mop floors 040
- ☐ Vacuum carpets and area rugs 052, 054
- ☐ Dust lampshades and chandeliers 065, 069

MONTHLY
- ☐ Clean mirrors 018
- ☐ Clean window treatments 019
- ☐ Wash trash cans 037
- ☐ Clean doorknobs 038

SEASONALLY (SPRING AND FALL)
- ☐ Wash windows 017
- ☐ Deep clean window treatments 019
- ☐ Wipe doors and baseboards 023
- ☐ Clean walls 026
- ☐ Clean exterior doors 035
- ☐ Deep clean lampshades 066
- ☐ Clean lamp bases and sconces 067, 068
- ☐ Clean chandeliers and light fixtures 069, 070

072 CARE FOR YOUR KITCHEN

It's the site of food preparation and consumption, home-work completion and minor injury triage, intimate conversation and coffee with your besties, so the kitchen must be presentable at all times. From wiping down surfaces every day to deep cleaning appliances seasonally, this section will help you navigate kitchen cleanup and make the process hassle free—or at least hassle friendly.

073 PICK A RUG

When choosing a kitchen mat or rug, opt for easy-to-clean materials, such as nylon, polyester, cotton, or polypropylene. They're the best at standing up to moisture, spills, and high traffic. There are also cushioned mats that wipe clean and skidproof mats that won't trip you up.

074 TRY SWEDISH DISHCLOTHS

Durable Swedish dishcloths are a smart alternative to paper towels and sponges. They're stiff when dry, but when they're wet, they're soft, spongy, and ultra-absorbent. They can be reused many times over, machine-washed, and then eventually composted.

075 REDUCE PAPER

Cut down on paper waste in your kitchen by replacing paper towels and napkins with cloth versions. In addition to being more eco-friendly than disposable products, they are also better for your budget. Keep a small basket in your kitchen—under the sink is a handy spot—for collecting kitchen laundry.

076 MIX IT IN THE KITCHEN

Keep your kitchen looking—and smelling—
fantastic with these simple, natural recipes
to create homemade cleaning supplies.

NOTE: Remember that while natural cleaners can be useful for cleaning and getting
that sparkle and shine, they don't quite cut it
for sanitizing germy surfaces. For that, turn
to an all-purpose cleaner. There are several
plant-based disinfectants that are effective
at killing bacteria and viruses.

ALL-PURPOSE CLEANER

2 tsp. borax

$\frac{1}{4}$ tsp. liquid castile soap

10 drops lemon essential oil

Mix all ingredients with hot water in a 16-oz. spray bottle.

NONABRASIVE VINEGAR CLEANER

1 part distilled white vinegar

2 parts water

5 drops essential oil

Combine the vinegar and water in a 16-oz. spray bottle. Add 5 drops of essential oil, such as lavender, grapefruit, orange, lemon, or peppermint, if you don't like the smell of vinegar.

GARBAGE DISPOSAL BOMBS

Makes 24 bombs.

$\frac{1}{2}$ c. citric acid

1 $\frac{1}{2}$ c. baking soda

30 drops orange essential oil

Mix all ingredients in a bowl until thoroughly combined. Use a spray bottle to mist just enough water for the mixture to hold its shape. Mold the mixture into small balls with a rounded tablespoon and place on a cookie sheet to dry overnight. Store in an airtight container.

DISINFECTANT

2 tbsp. liquid castile soap

20 drops tea tree oil

Mix the soap and essential oil with hot water in a 16-oz. spray bottle.

DRAIN CLEANER

1 c. table salt

1 c. baking soda

2–3 qt. water

1 c. distilled vinegar

Thoroughly mix the salt and baking soda in a small bowl. Boil the water in a kettle. Pour the salt and baking soda mixture down the drain, then slowly pour the vinegar into the drain. Let it bubble for 1 to 2 minutes. Clear the drain by pouring in the boiling water. Wipe the drain cover with a soft cloth to make sure no salt or vinegar remains.

077 SET UP RECYCLING

Most garbage comes from cooking and eating, so it's logical to establish a good recycling system in the kitchen. Get an extra container so you can quickly sort recycling from trash. If you have room, double waste bins, in which the recycling is right next to the trash, make recycling second nature. Tight on space? Try a countertop recycling bin near the sink for gathering recyclables that have just been washed. Here's a short list of items that are generally okay to recycle everywhere:

- Aluminum and tin cans
- #1 and #2 plastic containers (check the bottoms)
- Cereal and other food boxes (these used to be no-no's because of their waxy coating, but now are widely accepted)

078 DIY FOAMING HAND SOAP

Foaming hand soap has become hugely popular, in large part because it uses both less water and less soap. A little goes a long way, and if you already have an empty foaming soap dispenser, it's easy to whip up a lather at home. Pour 2 tbsp. of castile soap into the bottle. If you wish, add up to 10 drops of your favorite essential oil. Here's where you can customize it for the season! Then slowly add water to the bottle, being sure to leave space for the pump. Screw on the lid, and then then give it a swirl to mix everything together. For a moisturizing soap, add bit of sweet almond oil or olive oil.

079

GATHER THESE RECYCLABLES

When it comes to recycling, the material is more important than the form. You probably know the basics of what's acceptable recycling, but could be forgetting these things:

ALUMINUM FOIL It's the same as a can!

PLASTIC LINERS INSIDE FOOD BOXES Most are made from #2 plastic.

JUNK MAIL Just pull out pieces with plastic windows.

080

REUSE KITCHEN CANISTERS

Brighten up your windowsill with outdated kitchen canisters that have been repurposed as herb pots. Spray paint them for a fresh look, and then add chalkboard labels to mark the names of the plants.

081 REMOVE STICKY LABELS

Label-less glass jars have loads of potential to be reused, but getting rid of that gummy residue can be a headache. The most natural way to get rid of it is by simmering the bottles or jars in a pot filled $3/4$ of the way with water and a sprinkle of baking soda. After they've cooled, rub any remaining sticky spots with baking soda. For truly stubborn gunk or larger items, an adhesive remover such as Goo Gone will do the trick.

082 CLEAN YOUR COMPOST BIN

Composting is an eco-friendly habit that cuts down on waste, but a stinky container is a major deterrent. Here are a few tips to keep it from getting gross:

- Line the bottom of your container with newspaper to absorb moisture and odors.
- Use hot water, baking soda, and vinegar to clean and deodorize the container after emptying it. Take extra care to avoid soaps or chemicals, as they can disrupt the compost ecosystem.

083 KEEP PET BOWLS ORDERLY

Water drips and stray kibble often go hand in hand with being a pet parent. But water can damage floors and be a slipping hazard, and rogue pet food can attract pests and is revolting to clean up when it gets wet. Stay on top of your dog or cat's feeding station messes by putting the bowls on an elevated stand or a place mat that can go in the dishwasher. Under that you can layer a small rug to collect anything that flies out of the bowls. Finally, be sure you clean your pet's dishes daily or at least every couple of days. If you feed your pet raw food, it's critical that you wash the dishes twice a day to avoid harmful bacteria growth.

084 COMPLETE YOUR EVENING

It feels great to start the day with a clean kitchen, as it boosts your mood for the entire day. So, before going to bed, do a quick clean up. It should take no more than 15 minutes.

LOAD Fill the dishwasher and start it. Unload first thing in the morning.

WASH Clean anything that can't go in the dishwasher and set it all aside to air-dry.

CLEAN Rinse the sink, then sprinkle with baking soda and a squirt of castile soap. With a sponge, work it into a paste and let it sit while you clean the table, counters, and stove.

SPRAY Use the All-Purpose Cleaner (see tip 076) on tables, counters, and the stove, and wipe them down.

DRY Go back to the hand-washed pieces, dry with a towel if needed, and put them away.

RINSE Wash the baking soda paste off the sink and polish dry with a clean towel to prevent water spots.

SWEEP Use a broom and dustpan or vacuum to clean the floor.

FRESHEN Put out new washcloths and dish towels for the next day.

085 START FRESH

The kitchen is clean from the night before, so it's quick work to clean up after breakfast.

EMPTY Unload the dishwasher, which you filled and ran last night. With this routine, you'll never again wonder if dishes are clean or dirty.

LOAD Put breakfast dishes into the dishwasher. It only takes an extra minute or two!

WIPE Spray counters and the breakfast table with the All-Purpose Cleaner (see tip 076) and then wipe clean.

RINSE Use the spray nozzle to rinse the sink. Sprinkle some baking soda, work it in with a sponge, let it sit for a few minutes, then rinse again.

SWEEP Get those breakfast crumbs!

QUICK TIP

MAKE A BETTER FIT

Take advantage of adjustable shelves to customize for your bottles, jars, and jugs, and maximize every inch of fridge real estate.

RESET
THE FRIDGE

Plan on cleaning the fridge and freezer on your grocery-shopping day since it's more efficient to clean a near-empty fridge and freezer than one packed with supplies that you'll need to unload. Remove expired food, then quickly wipe down the shelves, walls, and drawers with the Nonabrasive Vinegar Cleaner (see tip 076).

Every six months, deep clean your refrigerator. Plan to do this before a major grocery restock because you'll need to completely empty both the refrigerator and freezer. And make sure to unplug the unit or turn the power off at the electrical panel before starting!

STEP ONE Empty the refrigerator and freezer, and use the frozen foods to protect perishable items by placing them all in a cooler. Put any other items on the nearest counter, organizing them by the drawer or shelf to which you plan to return them.

STEP TWO Wash shelves and let dry while you wipe the interior of the fridge. To thoroughly clean glass shelves and crisper drawers, use a mixture of 1 tbsp. dishwashing liquid and 2 c. Nonabrasive Vinegar Cleaning. Wash and replace shelf liners.

STEP THREE Soap is hard to rinse away from the interior walls of a refrigerator, so use a separate spray bottle of the dishwashing liquid/vinegar solution you made in Step Two and wipe the interior walls and door compartments. The solution will help remove lingering fridge odors as well as helping to prevent new ones.

STEP FOUR If a spot is still resistant, mix $1/2$ c. baking soda and 3 tbsp. water to create a baking soda paste and let it sit for 15 minutes, then scrub with a toothbrush. Wipe away the baking soda paste and residue.

STEP FIVE Before you put everything back, clean each jar and carton with a damp cloth so you don't end up putting sticky containers back on your newly clean shelves. While you're at it, check the expiration dates and toss any expired food items, along with anything you know you'll never cook with again.

STEP SIX Finally, add a new, open box of baking soda on a middle shelf to absorb future odors.

087 DESIGNATE ZONES

For speedy fridge clean-out and refilling, have a system for where things go. Don't feel beholden to where certain types of food should go. Instead, think about what you use every day, and keep it at eye level for easy access. Designate one shelf for leftovers and the bottom shelf for raw meat for food safety reasons.

088 SPLIT IT UP

When sharing a fridge with roommates, agree on separate areas for food you want to save for yourself and another zone for communal items, such as condiments.

089 UPCYCLE EGG CARTONS

Once the eggs have all been cooked, hold onto the paper egg cartons. They're ideal for cushioning fragile holiday ornaments, organizing small bits and bobs (such as paper clips, buttons, or screws), or as an eco-friendly alternative to packing peanuts as a shipping filler.

090 FREE UP THE FREEZER

If you have a freestanding freezer, follow the steps from tip 086 for cleaning the refrigerator. Unplug the unit or turn it off at the electrical panel before starting the process. Plan menus ahead and try to use as much as you can out of the freezer so there is less frozen food to remove and store when cleaning. Empty the freezer, throwing out food that has freezer burn or has been around too long.

091 DUST THE CONDENSER

Regular cleaning of the condenser coils on the back of fridges and freezers keeps them operating at maximum efficiency, reduces power usage, and extends the life of the unit. Manufacturers recommend cleaning the coils every 3 to 6 months, and more often if you have any pets.

READ Refer to the manufacturer's manual to locate the condenser and fan and review any specific warnings that may apply to your particular model.

REVEAL Use a flashlight to more easily spot any obscured patches of dust or cobwebs.

CLEAN Slide a refrigerator coil brush—a long, short-bristled tool—between coils to remove dust and fuzz. Work gently to avoid damage.

REMOVE Have the vacuum handy to remove dust and cobwebs from the coil brush as you work. Once finished with the refrigerator coil brush, you can vacuum the condenser with a crevice or dust-brush attachment, again working carefully. While the unit is away from the wall, remember to vacuum the exposed floor.

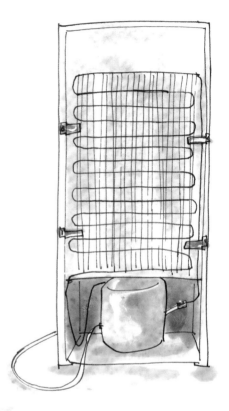

092 WIPE THE EXTERIOR

There are many different types of exterior finishes available for refrigerators and freezers: enamel, regular stainless steel, fingerprint-resistant stainless steel, wood veneer, and painted panels. Review the owner's manual for any special cleaning instructions. Cleaning these surfaces is easy to do. Simply wipe away the dirt and grime with a microfiber cloth dampened with soapy water, then rinse the cloth and wipe away any residue.

093 KEEP YOUR FRIDGE FRONT CLEAR

A refrigerator covered in magnets, papers, and pictures looks cluttered and is difficult to clean. If you have a good paper management system, you shouldn't need to rely on your fridge front for posting reminders. If there are some things that make the most sense to keep on your fridge—such as your weekly menu or grocery shopping list—keep it to the side of the fridge.

094 ABSORB FRIDGE ODORS

Baking soda is a go-to for keeping your fridge smelling fresh, but in disastrous cases—like when you lose power and your freezer full of seafood spoils—you need to pull out the big guns. It will take a little time, but luckily it's an easy fix. First, take care to clean your fridge or freezer very well with a disinfectant to eradicate any bacteria. Then, fill the appliance with crumpled-up newspaper. In a day or so they will have sucked up the stench. Replace the newspaper and repeat the process if any odors linger.

LINE THE FRIDGE

After each seasonal cleaning, finish by putting washable liners on all the shelves and in the drawers. When messes happen, simply take out the liner and wash it in the sink instead of removing an entire shelf or drawer.

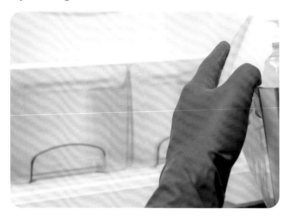

095

SHINE STAINLESS STEEL

To give stainless steel finishes a brilliant gleam, spray with the Nonabrasive Vinegar Cleaner (see tip 076) and wipe clean with a microfiber cloth. To remove streaks, apply baby oil to a microfiber cloth and wipe in the direction of the grain. Flip the cloth over and wipe one more time to polish it. Keep in mind that you need to avoid abrasive cleaning products, abrasive sponges, and steel wool, as they will permanently scratch stainless steel.

CLEAN
THE OVEN

If you have a self-cleaning oven, you can use that feature according to your oven's instructions. However, you will still want to clean the oven racks separately, as described below, because the very high temperature required for a self-cleaning oven can damage the racks. Some people prefer using nontoxic products that they mix themselves. As with all of your appliances, refer to the owner's manual for any specific do's and don'ts.

SOAK Remove the oven racks and then lay them on a towel in the bathtub so that the racks don't damage the tub's porcelain finish. Fill the tub with 6 to 8 in. of hot water and add 1/2 c. castile soap. Soak the racks overnight and then rinse thoroughly.

WIPE With the racks removed, give the oven a wipedown inside with a damp cloth to remove any loose crumbs.

MIX Make a paste out of baking soda and water (about 1 c. baking soda to 6 tbsp. water).

COAT If your oven has removable heating elements, take them out. Next, cover the entire oven—including the window—with the paste and let it sit in the cold oven for at least 6 hours. Avoid getting any paste on the electrical elements when applying it to the interior.

CLEAN Spread old towels on the floor in front of the oven to catch stray gunk. Using a moist sponge, wipe off the paste. Rinse the sponge often in clean water and continue to wipe up all vestiges of the baking soda paste. Keep a bucket of water nearby for convenient rinsing, but be sure to change the water often to keep the sponge clean. Spray any resistant patches of hardened spills with white vinegar, which will help dislodge them.

097
REUSE
HOT WATER

When you have a pot full of hot water ready to drain, take a second to think about what could use a good soak. Scalding water can be quite effective at loosening burnt-on bits from skillets or lifting debris from stovetop burners. Place grimy items in the bottom of your sink and pour the water right on top.

098
SWIPE DEBRIS

Before you turn on your oven for cooking, open the door and take a peek at the bottom of it. Crumbs can scorch and turn into a smoky mess if not addressed. A quick pickup or suck of the vacuum will keep the fumes at bay and deep cleanings more manageable.

QUICK TIP

WIPE UP SPILLS QUICKLY

When a blueberry cobbler overflows or the roasted chicken drips coming out of the oven, it is easier to wipe up the spill while it's still warm. Do wait for the oven to cool a bit so you don't burn yourself, but if possible, get to the spill before it cools and hardens.

099
LOOSEN OVEN
MESSES WITH STEAM

A natural and smoke-free way to clean your oven is with steam. Place an oven-safe pot or dish (a roasting pan works great) filled $^2/_3$ of the way with water on the bottom rack of your oven. Crank the heat to 450 degrees Fahrenheit (232 degress Celsius) and let the steam do its thing for about an hour. Once your oven has cooled, wipe off the condensation, grease, and grime.

100 GET A FRESH, CLEAN MICROWAVE

A boiling cup of lemon water will steam clean your microwave oven's interior. Here's how to get the best effect—and a lemony-fresh scent.

WIPE Do a quick clean-out of the microwave with a damp cloth and the Nonabrasive Vinegar Cleaner (see tip 076). Pick up loose crumbs and anything that will come up without effort.

MIX Slice a lemon in half and squeeze the juice from the lemon into a microwave-safe bowl. Add 1 c. water and add the lemon halves into the bowl as well.

BOIL Heat the bowl of lemon halves, juice, and water in the microwave for 3 to 5 minutes (depending on how dirty your microwave is). When the time is up, do not open the door. Let it sit for about 5 minutes more in order to steam and loosen grime inside the microwave.

FINISH Carefully remove the hot bowl and set it aside. Wipe the steamed microwave interior again. If there's a turntable or a tray, remove and wipe it as well. Go after stubborn spots with the lemon water and a cloth and then use the lemon water as a cleaning solution on the front of the microwave door and the keypad.

QUICK TIP

OUT OF LEMONS?

This technique also works with a splash of white vinegar. Heating it in a glass measuring cup makes it easy to safely remove from the microwave. Then, pour the hot vinegar water down your kitchen sink to help deodorize your drain.

101 MAINTAIN THE COOKTOP

Wiping the surface of the stove every evening takes no time at all. Even when a pot boils over or a sauce splashes, taking care of it right away makes it easier to clean. Waiting around just makes those splashes harder to clean up, especially if they accumulate. A daily cleaning of the surface also allows you to go longer between more thorough cleanups. By design, some cooktops are easier to clean, with sealed burners that help to prevent food falling into unreachable gaps and grates that can safely go into the dishwasher (remember that when you're shopping for a new one). Whether your stovetop or cooktop needs a thorough cleaning weekly or monthly will vary with its design and use.

102 MINIMIZE SPLATTERS

A spoon rest is a small kitchen accessory that makes a big difference in curtailing cooking messes. Having a handy spot to put down your utensils means you're less likely to plop it on the counter or stove. A dishwasher-safe version can get cleaned with your nightly load.

103 KEEP IT SIMPLE

Induction cooktops are the easiest to maintain, particularly if you wipe the smooth top right away with a damp microfiber cloth every time you cook. Any food left on the surface after cooking will soon harden from residual heat and can be tough to remove. The ceramic-glass surface is vulnerable to scratches, so avoid using any abrasive sponges or products to clean this cooktop.

To deal with hardened food, pour a little olive oil on the area to loosen the stain, then scrape with a ceramic-cooktop scraper or a paint scraper from the hardware store (hold it at a 40- to 45-degree angle to avoid scratching the glass). Wipe once with soapy water and then rinse with a clean sponge. If food still remains, apply a baking soda paste and let it sit for 10 minutes. Wipe again with soapy water and rinse well to remove all the baking soda paste.

104 MAKE ELECTRIC STOVES SPARKLE

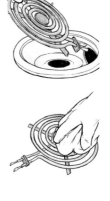

Cleaning an electric stovetop is similar to a gas one in several ways—you'll wipe the surface down the same, and you will be using the same techniques to clean the knobs and control panel (see tip 105). However, the electric coils require special care.

First, unplug the electric coils, which is often as simple as lifting them up and pulling them out. If they're dirty, you can put a little soapy water on a microfiber cloth and rub them clean. Never submerge the coils in water. Be careful to keep the electrical connection from getting wet.

With the coils off, lift the drip pans and soak them in hot, soapy water. If they are particularly dirty, make a paste of baking soda and water ($1/2$ c. baking soda and 3 tbsp. water) and wipe it on the drip pans, letting it sit for 30 minutes. Then scrub the drip pan with a nonabrasive sponge.

Once the coils and pans are clean, thoroughly dry them off—especially the coils—before reinstalling them.

105 CARE FOR GAS STOVES

Gas stoves require a little more effort to keep clean and function at their best. Before you begin, turn on the stove and note if any of the burner holes appear to be clogged (you'll be able to tell because the flames will be uneven). Turn off the burners and let them cool completely before you start cleaning.

CLEAN GRATES AND BURNER CAPS Remove the grates and the burner caps and soak them in hot, soapy water for 30 minutes to 1 hour while you're cleaning the rest of the stove. After soaking, use a toothbrush to scrub any cooked-on spots.

WIPE THE SURFACE Spray the top of the stove with the Nonabrasive Vinegar Cleaner (see tip 076) and wipe with a nonabrasive sponge or microfiber cloth. Add 1 tbsp. mild soap to the Nonabrasive Vinegar Cleaner and scrub with a toothbrush if the spot is stubborn. Then spray with clean water and wipe it off using a dry cloth.

CLEAR THE CRUMBS Gas ranges often include a way to remove crumbs and crud that have fallen below the burner units. With the grates removed, you may be able to lift the top (like the hood of a car) to clean below. There may also be a tray that pulls out from your range. In either case, take advantage of its easy access and periodically clean it.

CLEAN KNOBS Remove the knobs and wipe with the Nonabrasive Vinegar Cleaner and a microfiber cloth. Before replacing the knobs, remember to clean the control panel itself. Thoroughly dry the grates and burner caps, then return them back to their proper place.

HANDLE BURNER HEADS Remove the burner heads, which diffuse the flow of gas through holes in their exterior rim. The best way to spot a clogged hole is when the gas is lit. You don't want to handle a hot burner head, so test and note the flames an hour or so ahead of time. It's common for a white, powdery buildup to collect around the dispersal holes. This can be easily cleared with a pin or paper clip. If heavier cleaning is needed, soak the heads in hot, soapy water for 30 minutes. It's critical that they dry completely in a oven set on "low" for 30 minutes before replacing! (This is a good time to consult the owner's manual, as the head will sit level and operate only in the right position.)

106 DON'T FORGET THE VENT HOOD

The overhead vent above your cooktop absorbs grease and smoke every time it's turned on, which means that its filters need a good cleaning every 3 to 6 months. You can clean the filters on the low-heat cycle of your dishwasher, but they usually have so much collected grease that it's best to wash them without other dishes in the cycle. If you wash them by hand, a long soak is recommended.

STEP ONE Spray an appropriate cleaning solution on the surface panels of the vent hood. Depending on the surface material, choose either the Nonabrasive Vinegar Cleaner (see tip 076), a mild soap solution, or follow guidelines for stainless steel (see tip 095). Wipe clean with a microfiber cloth. If you have not done this in a while, ready yourself for the collected grime and resolve to clean the hood more often!

STEP TWO Remove the filters and put them in the sink or bathtub, or someplace else large

enough to submerge them in water. Sprinkle $\frac{1}{2}$ c. baking soda on top of the filters and fill the sink or tub with scalding water (from the tap or boiled in a kettle). Let the filters soak for a few minutes to help break up any caked-on grease. After soaking, scrub lightly and persistently with a soft-bristled brush that will not damage the delicate filters in the hood.

STEP THREE Rinse with water and let the filters air-dry. Put them back in the vent hood after they have completely dried out.

WASH BY HAND

Proclamations on what should and should not be washed in a dishwasher are a surefire way to start an argument between the closest of friends. The truth is that all dishwashers are not created equal, so what works for you may not work for others. Below are items that should always be washed by hand to avoid even a chance of damage, or are worth a few minutes of extra effort.

MATERIAL	WASHING DIRECTIONS
FINE CHINA AND CRYSTAL	They are delicate and deserve to be treated as such. Gilded edges absolutely should not be in the dishwasher, where they will darken and discolor.
WOODEN COOKING UTENSILS AND CUTTING BOARDS	Rinse them by hand and apply baking soda to eliminate stains from beets, strawberries, cherries, and other foods.
KITCHEN KNIVES	The heat and detergent will dull knife blades and may loosen the handles. Better to wipe them clean and dry them after use, immediately storing them in a knife slot where the blade is protected.
SILVERWARE	Attitudes about putting silverware in the dishwasher have relaxed over time. It's up to you how careful you want to be with your silverware. Hand-wash if that ritual is important to you. It's okay to put silverware in the dishwasher, but make certain that none of your everyday stainless flatware comes in contact. The stainless will scratch and discolor the softer silver.
PLASTIC UTENSILS AND STORAGE CONTAINERS	Hand-washing is better, but washing on the top shelf of the dishwasher is usually safe for most plastics.
SILVER SERVICE PIECES	Silver service dishes risk getting beat up in the dishwasher, so wash them by hand in hot, sudsy water as soon as guests leave and dry with a soft towel. Foods with salt, mayonnaise, and eggs will discolor silver if left to dry, and soaking in water overnight will also damage the silver. Give them immediate attention!
CAST IRON SKILLETS AND POTS	Sprinkle a generous covering of salt on the interior surface and rub it in with a plastic scrubber. The salt absorbs grease and food without using water, which will rust cast iron. It's okay to then lightly rinse with warm water, but thoroughly dry to avoid rusting. If you rinse with water, apply a thin coat of vegetable oil and wipe with a paper towel to protect the seasoned finish before storing.
NONSTICK COOKWARE	Manufacturers recommend whether or not to put their nonstick pans in the dishwasher, but if you're particular about their care, wash them by hand.
COPPER POTS AND PANS	Copper will lose its luster in the dishwasher. Instead, hand-wash in warm, soapy water. If food is baked on, soak the pan in water until the food loosens. Avoid scrubbing!
EVERYDAY POTS AND PANS	Assuming you've been filling the dishwasher since breakfast, there may not be a lot of room left. Pots and pans, even if they are dishwasher safe, take up a lot of space, and crusted food doesn't always get effectively cleaned in the dishwasher. Take a few minutes to hand-wash them.

108 REMOVE RUST FROM CAST IRON

If you do end up with rust spots on your cast iron cookware, you only need two ingredients to get it back to tip-top shape: coarse salt and a potato. Cut a potato in half. Sprinkle coarse salt onto the rust, and then use the potato to rub it in. Keep going, adding more salt as needed until the pan is rust free. Rinse the pan clean, and then heat and re-season the cast iron.

WASH MORE
EFFICIENTLY

Although there's not really a wrong way to wash dishes by hand, there may be a better way than your current system. Increasing your efficiency will save time and energy better spent on other things.

SOAK Fill your sink or a large rubber basin with hot, sudsy water and let your dishes soak for a few minutes. A little bit of soaking can help loosen stuck-on food, especially greasy residues and dried-up food particles.

SELECT Choose a type of item to wash and tackle the entire group, rather than randomly selecting items. Whether you start with dishes, bowls, cups, or flatware, similar items will fit more efficiently in your dish rack.

WASH Scrub the food off your dishes in the soapy water so the water can help separate loosened food from the dishes. Use the hottest water your hands can handle.

RINSE When finished—or at least finished with a batch that fills your basin—dump the dirty water and start rinsing the dishes with the rinse water collecting in the basin. If all the dishes are washed and in the basin, the collecting rinse water will further help dislodge the food you loosened with the wash sponge. If you have another batch to do, add dish soap to the collected rinse water to continue the process.

DRY Allow your dishes to sit, even for a minute, so excess water can drip into the dish drainer instead of prematurely saturating your dish towel.

REPLACE Another benefit of washing in item groups is how you can efficiently put them away in one place, rather than having to move back and forth to different cabinets and drawers.

110 TEAM UP

When living with others, there's no reason one person needs to be solely responsible for washing dishes. Share the burden by designating one person to wash and another to dry and put away. The task will go much more quickly and feels way less daunting.

111 CLEAN YOUR DRYING RACK

Your dish drainer can become a breeding ground for bacteria and smells, especially if you keep it out on your counter or in your sink, where it can get splashed or splattered while cooking and cleaning. After you put your clean dishes away, dry the dish drainer off well, and don't forget the drip tray beneath it if there is one. Once a week, run it through the dishwasher for a good sanitizing. If it's made of bamboo, wash by hand with hot water and soap instead.

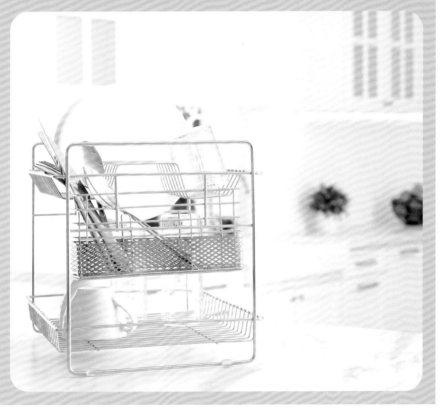

112 DISMISS DRIPS

Stuck wondering where to place that just-washed slow-cooker insert, cutting board, or cast iron pan? They'd topple your drying rack or immediately drench your dish towel. This is when a drying mat comes in handy. Often made of microfiber, these super-absorbent mats soak up water. They're usually cushioned, as well, to protect delicate dishware.

113

CLEAN THE DISHWASHER

You depend on your dishwasher to do the workhorse job of cleaning your dirty dishes, glasses, flatware, casseroles, and pots. But it will need regular cleaning itself, too. Have a look at tips 114–122 and remember these easy steps to ensure that every load of dishes comes out sparkling clean from a pristine dishwasher.

114 WIPE THE EXTERIOR

Daily, if necessary, wipe around the controls and handle of your dishwasher. If you have a wooden or painted decorative panel on the front, use a barely dampened cloth to wipe it down. For stainless steel, clean with a microfiber cloth and the Nonabrasive Vinegar Cleaner (see tip 076). Next, apply baby oil to a microfiber cloth and wipe in the direction of the grain. Flip the cloth over and wipe one more time to finish polishing it.

115 LEARN TO LOAD

Modern dishwashers are engineered to do a superior job of cleaning and sanitizing compared to washing by hand, and with less wasted water. If dinnerware isn't coming out clean and you've given the machine a deep cleanse (see tip 120), it could be human error in loading the dishwasher. How you place your things in the dishwasher can make a difference in how clean they get: position each piece so that water can reach it, and avoid overcrowding that may chip, break, or scratch when pieces jostle during the cycle.

116 HAND-WASH TRAVEL MUGS

Very few travel mugs are dishwasher safe because water can get trapped between the inner and outer layers of insulation. Mold can grow there, as well as around the rubber seals on the lids. Wash them in a sink with warm water and dish soap.

117 SCRUB WATER BOTTLES

Although some plastic and stainless-steel water bottles are dishwasher safe, their no-spill straw and lid systems need extra attention. It's best to scrub the whole kit and caboodle by hand using a bottle brush, wire straw brush, and dishwashing liquid. Another option is to fill it halfway with a fifty–fifty mix of water and vinegar. Tighten the cap, shake well, then let it sit overnight. The next morning, rinse it well and let it dry.

118 ELIMINATE FOGGINESS

Cloudy drinking glasses develop over time when they're washed in a dishwasher instead of by hand. If you have hard water, then soak the glasses in vinegar for 15 minutes to get rid of the hazy film caused by mineral buildups. If the film remains, your glasses are probably permanently etched by soft-water corrosion, and there's no fix.

119 BANISH ODORS

Once a month, pour 1 c. white vinegar into the bottom of the empty dishwasher and set it to run through a heavy wash cycle. Vinegar cuts grease, deodorizes, and sanitizes. For extra freshening power, sprinkle 1 c. baking soda in the bottom of the dishwasher and run through a second, light cycle.

120 DEEP CLEAN

Every 6 months, the dishwasher and filter need a serious cleaning. Repeat the process more often if dishes and glasses just don't appear as clean as you like them—you may even save yourself the cost of a repairman's visit. Although soaking may extend the total time, your active time should be less than an hour.

STEP ONE Remove the racks and the flatware bin.

STEP TWO Remove the filter. Most are easy to remove, but consult the owner's manual if you're uncertain how to get it off. Clean with soapy water and scrub with a toothbrush if food is caught in the mesh cover.

STEP THREE Fill the sink with water and add 2 c. vinegar. Put the filter and the racks into the water and soak for at least an hour and as long as overnight. For racks too big to fit in the sink, soak them in the bathtub.

STEP FOUR Clear holes in the spinning arm that appear to be blocked. Use a toothpick or fine wire to open each hole, working carefully.

STEP FIVE Dampen a cloth with a solution of equal parts vinegar and water and wipe the interior surfaces before putting the filter, racks, and flatware bin back in.

121 MIND THE FLOW

Whether you're placing items on the top or bottom rack of the dishwasher, place the dirty side toward the center and down, facing the rotating arms that circulate the water. Pay attention to anything that might block the water flow. For instance, tall dinner plates, trays, and large casserole dishes should go on the outer edges of the rack. After loading, spin the arm to make certain nothing is blocking it. And don't put anything toward the front that would block the detergent dispenser! Plates and bowls that are vertically stacked will need space between them so the water can get to their surfaces. The racks that have vertical tines are designed to leave space around items as long as you don't overcrowd the dishes as you load them. The upper rack is often more open for free-form loading of small bowls, cups, and glasses.

Don't let pieces touch, which can restrict adequate water flow and risk breakage from vibrations during the wash cycle. Set cups and mugs at an angle so that their handles don't protrude. Overloading the washer might seem like you're saving time and water, but you could end up having to rewash any pieces that didn't get clean the first time around.

122 TRUST THE POWER

It isn't necessary to prerinse dishes in the sink, but you should scrape leftover food off that may clog the drain to the disposal. Also remove proteins, such as eggs and cheese, right away since they can harden on the plate as they sit.

PACK YOUR BASKET Manufacturers recommend loading flatware with the handles down for the most efficient cleaning. The exceptions are meat forks, knives, and any sharp utensil, which should be placed with the sharp end down to avoid accidental cuts. Make sure spoons and forks do not nest inside one another and block water from reaching them. Most baskets have an optional slotted screen that will hold the pieces away from each other during the wash cycle. When you've got a lot of flatware to load, put the screen in place first and fit individual pieces in through the slots.

USE ALL CYCLES Make use of the various settings to boost cleaning, conserve energy, and tailor the cycle to the load. If you don't yet have a full load, run a rinse cycle rather than letting food harden on the dishes.

 ## KNOW
YOUR SINK

Much like carpets and countertops, your sink's composition dictates the best course of action for cleaning. Its properties also present unique vulnerabilities, so use the suggested cleaning-solution recipes in this book. If your sink is smelly, use the Drain Cleaner to freshen it up (see tip 076).

MATERIAL	DAILY	TIPS & TRICKS	AVOID
STAINLESS STEEL	Rinse, then sprinkle with baking soda. Spray with the Nonabrasive Vinegar Cleaner (see tip 076), scrub with a sponge, then rinse again. Avoid water spots by drying the sink with a towel.	Occasionally wipe the sink with a little olive oil on a cloth to restore its shine.	Ammonia and bleach, as well as any abrasive cleaners and rough scrubbing pads.
PORCELAIN ENAMEL OVER CAST IRON	Clean after each use with mild dishwashing liquid and hot water. Rinse and dry.	Sprinkle baking soda on stains, and scrub with the cut side of a lemon. Rinse and dry.	Immediately remove tea bags, coffee, blueberries, red wine, mayonnaise, mustard, and pickles, or risk taking on permanent stains.
FIRECLAY	Clean with the Nonabrasive Vinegar Cleaner. Dry with a towel to prevent water spots.	Sprinkle baking soda on resistant stains. Scrub with a soft sponge. Rinse and dry.	Harsh scouring powders and commercial drain cleaners.
SOLID SURFACE	Clean with warm, soapy water and a sponge, then rinse and dry. Treat with the Disinfectant (see tip 076) after raw meat or poultry has been in the sink.	Use a nonscratch scrubber with baking soda or vinegar to get rid of stains.	Water that dries on the surface creates an unsightly film, so dry often. And remember, hot pots and pans can scorch.
COMPOSITE GRANITE AND COMPOSITE QUARTZ	Use only mild soap (pH neutral) and a soft cloth. Rinse well and dry with a towel after every use.	Reseal the sinks annually to minimize staining.	Food stains and hard water can permanently etch the surface. Citrus, vinegar, and ammonia can strip the finish.
ACRYLIC COMPOSITE	Use mild soap and water, and always rinse well. Dry with a towel after each use to avoid water spotting.	On stains only, use the Nonabrasive Vinegar Cleaner.	Abrasives will scratch the surface and hot pots will scorch.
SOAPSTONE	Scrub with a mild soap and sponge to diminish the white haze that often develops with hard water. Rinse well to remove soap and dry.	Every 4 to 6 weeks, rub olive oil into the stone. Let it absorb for 30 minutes to 1 hour, then buff dry.	Abrasives will scratch the surface, and lemon juice and vinegar will etch the stone.
COPPER	Wash with mild soap and a sponge. Rinse well, and dry off the metal using a microfiber cloth.	Most new copper sinks have an applied patina that will be damaged by abrasive scrubbing.	Acidic foods (citrus, tomatoes, and vinegar) will pit the surface. Abrasive scrubbers will scratch.

124 TRY A CADDY

Corral your cleaning essentials, such as your sponge and dish brush, in a sink caddy. Stainless steel wire sink baskets allow for plenty of airflow. Opt for a style that rests over your sink divider rather than the kind that attaches with plastic suction cups, as those tend to get gross quickly.

125 RECHARGE THE DISPOSAL

A garbage disposal takes only a little care to operate efficiently, banishing smells and keeping the drains clear.

FRESHEN WITH CITRUS Anytime you cook or eat a lemon or orange, drop in a few peels when you run the disposal. Once a week, put a citrus wedge or a Garbage Disposal Bomb (see tip 076) into the disposal and run it with cold water for a few seconds to clean the blades and freshen the space.

DEEP CLEAN Every two weeks put $^1/_2$ c. baking soda down the disposal. Chase it with 1 c. vinegar. It will fizz just like a middle-school science project, killing some bacteria in the disposal and drain. But more importantly, the minute bubbling will help dislodge bits of food and muck that have gotten caught in this dangerous and hard-to-reach place. Leave it for 10 minutes before pouring a kettle full of boiling water down the drain.

ICE IT DOWN During spring and fall, dump a tray full of ice cubes down the disposal, follow with a cup of rock salt, then turn on the cold water and the disposal. The whirling blades of the disposal will turn the ice and rock salt into a blizzard of shrapnel, scouring the walls that you can't reach while also cleaning the blades.

126 MAINTAIN YOUR DISPOSAL

Always run cold water before, during, and after the disposal is switched on and off. This serves three purposes: It helps shift food around inside the disposal to maximize the chances it will get chopped up; flowing water will help push the food particles through your pipes, decreasing the chance of clogs; and cold water solidifies any foodstuff that liquefies when hot such as oil and cheese. It's better to have small, solid chunks go through your disposal than liquids that may cool into a coating, or solidify into a blockage down the line. Never put chemicals such as bleach or drain cleaners in the disposal. They can damage the blades, rubber and plastic parts, and the plumbing.

Don't overload a disposal. Give it time to process and clear smaller handfuls before adding more.

If a clog occurs, unplug the disposal or turn it off at the electrical panel. Never try to unclog it while it's attached to its power source, even if no one else is around to accidentally turn on the activation switch.

If it stops while still partially filled, use kitchen tongs to remove the food. If fibrous strings or a stray rubber band gets wrapped around the blades, remove them with needle-nose pliers. Be very careful when putting any tools in the cavity.

KEEP IT CLEAR

Some foods should never be put into a disposal because they risk either clogging the drains or damaging the disposal's mechanics. The list below should go into the compost or trash.

TRASH

Grease and Fat Pour bacon grease, oil discarded after frying or sautéing, and other fats into empty bottles with caps; toss when the bottle is full.

Bones They'll dull the disposal blades and clog the plumbing, and shards could be propelled out of the hole.

Pasta and Rice With exposure to water in the disposal, they will expand and solidify in the pipes beyond the disposal, resulting in a glob that won't allow water through.

COMPOST

Eggshells They don't completely break down in the disposal and can clog plumbing.

Fruit Pits and Seeds Hard pits and even small seeds are just too hard for the small blades of a disposal.

Celery, Kale, Rhubarb Tough, fibrous foods can get wrapped around the disposal blades, inhibiting their movement.

Potato and Carrot Peels Whenever there are a lot of vegetable peels, they clump into a paste, making it hard for the disposal to keep up with the volume and risking a clog or shutdown.

Onion and Garlic Skins Bulb skins are too thin to break down in the blades and often cling to the walls of the disposal.

128 CARE FOR FAUCETS

A quick, daily towel wipe will keep your sink hardware looking like new. Most kitchen faucets, handles, and other built-in sink accessories installed within the last 20 years have a factory-applied coating that is stain and tarnish resistant. You only need to wipe the hardware with a soft cloth after every use to remove fingerprints and water spotting. Be diligent because minerals in the water and soap scum that are left to sit will wear away the protective coating over time.

PROTECT THE COATING Your goal is to preserve the faucet's protective coating because if the coating is scratched or chipped, the base material is exposed to oxidization and can discolor. Stay away from abrasive cleaners and cleaning pads, bleach, ammonia, rubbing alcohol, acidic solutions, cleaning products designed to remove tarnish or rust, and polishes with harsh chemicals. Multiple manufacturers use an incredibly thin physical vapor deposition process or clean protective coated finishes on fixtures of brass, copper, bronze, stainless, chrome, or nickel, so it may be impossible to identify whether an existing fixture is coated or not.

PLAY IT SAFE If you can identify the manufacturer, check their website for specific cleaning instructions. If you're cleaning blind and want to remove accumulated water spots or soap, start with warm, soapy water, rinse well to remove all traces of soap, dry, and buff with a microfiber cloth. A soft toothbrush can get at dirt that may build up at the joints.

129 ENJOY LIVING FINISHES

Uncoated brass, copper, and bronze are known as "living" finishes, which beautifully change over time. These are prized for the patina they develop with age and wear; just keep water spots and soap scum off of them.

130 CLEAN OLDER FAUCETS RIGHT

Older, uncoated fixtures can be scratched by abrasive scrubbers, so only use soft cloths and sponges. Try these steps to maintain vintage faucets and knobs.

STEP ONE Start with soapy water, wiping with a soft cloth, rinse well, dry, and buff.

STEP TWO Use the Nonabrasive Vinegar Cleaner (see tip 076), wiping with a microfiber cloth.

STEP THREE Baking soda is a mild abrasive and is the next possibility. Sprinkle baking soda and let it sit for 5 minutes, rinse well, dry, and buff. Repeat this step if you're beginning to see results.

STEP FOUR For really grungy fixtures, use the Nonabrasive Vinegar Cleaner to make a baking soda paste and apply for 5 minutes. Rinse, dry, and buff.

131 CLEAN SEALED COUNTERTOPS

Stone countertops have a beautiful mix of colors and patterns—the natural swirls of marble, the magnificent speckling of granite, the subtle color shades and embedded fossils of limestone, and the randomness of cured concrete are all visually interesting. But that beauty comes at a cost: The porous nature of these stones make them extremely vulnerable to stains. They must be resealed annually to retain a semblance of stain resistance. But even sealed, these countertops are delicate and can be damaged, so keep these care tips in mind.

AVOID Acidic foods like citrus, tomatoes, red and white wine, tea, and coffee can compromise the sealant and chemically etch the surface. Abrasive cleaners, hot pans, and vinegar-based solutions can also damage the surface.

WASH Water with a little dish soap and a microfiber cloth are all you need for daily cleaning, but remember to dry with a clean cloth to avoid water spots.

APPLY If a stain does appear, rub in a paste of baking soda and water, cover with plastic wrap, seal the edges with tape, and leave in place for 24 hours—the baking soda paste will help draw out the stain. After the sitting period, wipe with soapy water, rinse with clean water, and dry well.

RESEAL Most penetrating sealants are simple to use. They usually need a thorough cleaning before applying the sealant, as well as time for the sealant to seep into the surface. Make sure to check instructions to ensure proper protection.

BAMBOO Give this surface a daily dusting followed by a wipe with a damp cloth. For deeper cleaning, start with soapy water. Stains can be treated with a thick salt paste and rubbed with a nonabrasive sponge. Rinse well and repeat as necessary.

BUTCHER BLOCK Wipe with the Nonabrasive Vinegar Cleaner (see tip 076)—be sure not to saturate and risk warping—and dry with a microfiber cloth. For fresh stains, sprinkle some salt on the stain and scrub with the cut side of a lemon half, let rest for a few minutes, then lightly rinse with water and dry. A food-safe oil applied every six months will help protect porous butcher block.

CERAMIC TILE Acid-based cleaners and aggressive scrubbing can dull a tile's glossy finish. Simply wipe with soapy water and microfiber cloth, dry, and buff with a dry towel to preserve the shine. Sanitize the grout once a week by spraying with the Disinfectant (see tip 076), letting it sit for a few minutes, then scrubbing with a grout brush or toothbrush. Rinse with hot water and dry with a microfiber cloth.

COMPOSITE QUARTZ Don't let spills dry; a damp microfiber cloth will do the trick, followed by a rinse with clean water and drying to avoid water spots. If food does dry on quartz, carefully scrape it away with the bowl of a plastic spoon and wipe with a nonabrasive sponge, soap, and water.

LAMINATE Wipe with soapy water and a microfiber cloth for daily cleaning or a little baking soda and water on a soft-bristled brush for a deep clean.

LAVA STONE Clean this surface with the All-Purpose Cleaner (see tip 076) and a microfiber cloth and spray with the Disinfectant weekly.

PAPER Countertops made from recycled paper are available in a range of sealed and unsealed finishes that necessitate different deep cleaning methods. Start with a daily wash with soapy water and consult the directions for your specific type of finish to determine how to tackle stains.

RECYCLED GLASS Wipe with soapy water and immediately remove any acidic foods like citrus if the glass is suspended in acrylic. For glass in a cement binder, follow the directions in tip 131.

SLATE AND SOAPSTONE These nonporous stones just need wiping with soapy water and a rinse.

SOLID SURFACE Also known as Corian and other brand-specific names, solid surfaces just need a little soapy water for most messes. Rub a baking soda paste on tough stains, rinse, and wipe dry.

STAINLESS STEEL Spray with the Nonabrasive Vinegar Cleaner and wipe with the grain using a microfiber cloth. Abrasive sponges and cleaners will scratch the surface. For stains, gently rub a baking soda paste with the grain, then rinse and dry with a microfiber cloth.

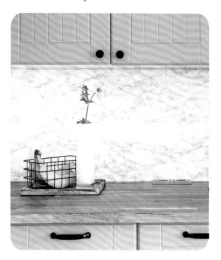

133 CLEAN COUNTER STOOLS

Many kitchens have islands or counters with stools for sitting and eating. They can be absolute magnets for drips, crumbs, and smudges. The material will dictate the best way to get them clean, but the best way to start is with a quick vacuum and wipe-down with a damp microfiber cloth to grab any loose debris. For fabric-upholstered stools, spot-treat them according to the care tag. Most wood stools can be cleaned with water and mild dish soap. Leather stools are durable and easy to clean; simply wipe with a damp cloth. For a more thorough cleaning, saddle soap is tops.

134 GET RID OF FRUIT FLIES

These pests seem to appear overnight when there's a piece of overripe fruit or empty bottle of wine left out. Banish the little buggers with a DIY trap. Mix equal parts apple cider vinegar and dish soap in a mason jar or teacup. Cover the top with plastic wrap, and then use a toothpick to poke holes in the plastic wrap. The flies will be attracted to the liquid, but unable to escape to breed.

135 LIFT AND WIPE

Move anything that sits on your countertop—the electric kettle, fruit bowl, blender, etc.—to thoroughly clean underneath and behind them. Crumbs have a way of collecting right beneath the edges of these items. You may realize that these, too, need a wipedown. They can get greasy or sticky from regular cooking. If you notice anything is dusty, it may be a sign that you don't use it frequently enough to warrant counter space.

136 THINK IN ZONES

As you're organizing your kitchen, or whenever you clear your counters for a good scrub, think about the smartest way to return the remaining items. For example, place your flour and sugar canisters near the cabinet where you store your mixer and measuring cups.

137 WASH BOARDS

Cutting boards protect your counters from cuts, but they are even more essential for protecting your family from food-borne illnesses. A good rule of thumb is to use two cutting boards: a wooden one for fruit, vegetables, and bread; and a plastic cutting board for meat. Never cut raw meat on a wooden board, because bacteria can leach into the wood, leading to cross-contamination of the next thing you cut on the same board.

HAND-WASH THE WOOD Dishwashers generate heat and steam that can warp and split wood, so always hand-wash wooden cutting boards. Scrub a wooden board with a stiff brush and soapy water, then spray it with the Nonabrasive Vinegar Cleaner (see tip 076) and let it sit a few minutes. Vinegar goes a long way toward killing household germs, bacteria, mold, and mildew. Rinse well with water and let it air-dry. Make sure it's completely dry because any moisture will encourage the growth of bacteria.

PUT PLASTIC IN THE DISHWASHER Plastic cutting boards benefit from a run through the dishwasher because of its high heat and strong detergent. First, rinse and scrub the board to

dispose of any bits of food and bacteria. These boards are very easy to clean, but they also become compromised with general use and knife marks that create openings for bacteria. You should replace them every few years. You may need to remove your plastic cutting board from the dishwasher before the drying cycle as it may warp with heat. Check the care instructions when purchasing.

QUICK TIP

TRY A TRAY

Corral smaller items, such as olive oil, the pepper grinder, or a salt pig, on a small dish or tray. Visually, it keeps your kitchen looking tidy and makes it a cinch to pick it up and transfer to another spot when cleaning.

138 LIFT STAINS WITH LEMON

When your wooden cutting board looks like it needs a little extra TLC, give it a good scrubdown by sprinkling it with coarse salt and then rub it with the cut side of a lemon half.

139 OIL YOUR BOARDS

Maintain your wooden cutting boards with semi-annual oiling. After they're clean and dry, give them a good rubdown with a food-grade oil, such as mineral oil or pure tung oil, and then let them sit overnight. The next morning, buff any residual oil with a soft cloth.

140 REFRESH THE COFFEE MAKER

Despite the fact that boiling water and abrasive coffee grounds are part of every cup of coffee, the coffee maker still needs a good scrub—it can grow more mold and bacteria than you want to imagine. Just clean it monthly for peace of mind and better tasting coffee! Here's how to clean a standard drip machine. (For instructions on your restaurant-grade espresso machine or Keurig, consult the owner's manual.)

STEP ONE Rinse the carafe and permanent filter with warm, soapy water. Spray the exterior of the machine with the Nonabrasive Vinegar Cleaner (see tip 076) and wipe off old stains.

STEP TWO Mix equal parts vinegar and water in the carafe and pour into the water dispenser. Put a paper filter or permanent filter in place to catch any debris, and start the brew cycle.

STEP THREE Halfway through the cycle, turn it off for an hour, then turn it back on to finish the brew cycle.

STEP FOUR Rinse the carafe and fill the water dispenser with plain water. Start another brew cycle. If you still smell vinegar, run a third cycle with more clean water.

141 CLEAN YOUR GRINDER

Whether you use it for coffee beans, spices, or both, your grinder can get a buildup of oils that can affect the flavors over time. Start fresh by grinding uncooked rice or some plain white bread in it. After a minute or so, dump out the rice flour or breadcrumbs and wipe it out with a damp paper towel.

142 REUSE COFFEE GROUNDS

Instead of dumping the grounds from your daily pot of coffee in the garbage can, extend their usefulness:

- Add them to your compost pile, where they will help food break down quickly.
- Keep a small dish of them near your sink and use them to get rid of garlic, onion, or seafood smells when washing your hands.
- Place a small bowl of dry coffee grounds in a musty cabinet or in your fridge to absorb unpleasant odors.

143 CLEAN YOUR KNIFE BLOCK

Although you clean your knives every time you use them, what about the knife block? Dust and crumbs accumulate in its slots. Periodically turn the vacuum on "high" suction and hold it over the slots. Clean the exterior as you would a wooden cutting board (see tip 137).

144 SHARPEN YOUR KNIVES

When your knives are dull, they're not worthless; they just need a good sharpening. Slide the knife blade through a manual knife sharpener or swipe the blade at an angle against a honing steel. If this makes you nervous, or you have a bunch of knives to sharpen, you can take them to a pro. (It's not as expensive as you might think!) Same goes for kitchen tools like vegetable peelers and graters.

145 TEND TO A TOASTER OVEN

Cleaning a toaster oven is pretty straightforward. Unplug it and take out all racks and trays (particularly the crumb tray on the bottom). Dump any loose debris and soak the racks and trays in hot soapy water. Spray the interior and exterior with the Nonabrasive Vinegar Cleaner (see tip 076) and wipe with a damp cloth.

146 PROCESS THE PROCESSOR

Cleaning the food processor is a quick task that's important to take care of every time you use it. Remove the bowl, blade, and other accessories and empty the bowl. Soak all in warm, soapy water. After 10 minutes, scrub with a microfiber cloth or sponge. Spray the motor base of the machine with the Nonabrasive Vinegar Cleaner (see tip 076), and wipe with a microfiber cloth. Dry all of the elements and put the processor back together.

147 BE GOOD TO YOUR BLENDER

Basic blender maintenance is simple and satisfying. Start off by pouring very hot water into the blender jar. Then add 2 squirts of dishwashing liquid, put the lid on, and blend for 10 to 15 seconds. Pour out the dirty water, rinse it well, and dry.

DEEP CLEAN If you use your blender for daily smoothies or pureed soups, you should take it apart once a week and soak the removable rubber gasket and the blade. Give the rest of the blender base a quick spray of the Nonabrasive Vinegar Cleaner (see tip 076) and wipe clean with a microfiber cloth.

148 HANDLE HIGH-PERFORMANCE BLENDERS

A new generation of more powerful blenders has surfaced with the desire for health-conscious smoothies. It takes a motor with higher horsepower to shear kale and other tough produce into a drinkable liquid, and these motors are designed to last a lifetime. Clean the containers and accessories well so they will last a lifetime, too.

Refer to your owner's manual before cleaning for the first time. Some containers, lids, and blades can go on the top rack of the dishwasher, but manufacturers may advise against putting any part in the dishwasher.

DAILY Leaving food to dry in the blender can damage the blades and the container, but a quick clean after each use is easy. Rinse the container in warm—not hot—water. Fill the blender jar no more than halfway with water and add only a drop or two of dishwashing soap. Let it run for 30 to 60 seconds; rinse again and air-dry.

MONTHLY Every month or two, fill half the jar with vinegar and add enough water to reach the top. Let that soak for half a day. Rinse and repeat cleaning with soapy water as described above.

DEEP CLEAN If your blender sees everyday use, you may begin to see a cloudy film inside the container. Minerals from fruits and vegetables are to blame, but you can get rid of the film. Pour 1 c. white vinegar into the container and fill it with water, leaving it to soak for several hours or overnight. If needed, use a soft scrubber on the inside, while taking care around the sharp edges of the blades.

149 JUICE IT

Electric juicers are designed for easy cleaning, but the following steps should be taken every time they're used:

STEP ONE Unplug the machine and disassemble all removable parts.

STEP TWO Empty the pulp and seeds into the compost.

STEP THREE Rinse all detachable accessories and soak them in warm, soapy water.

STEP FOUR Use a toothbrush to reach tight spots and to clean a mesh strainer. If the mesh strainer still has debris, add baking soda to the soap and water solution and let it soak for an additional 10 minutes.

STEP FIVE Rinse with clean water, air-dry, and reassemble.

150 DECLUTTER YOUR CABINETS

Gain valuable cooking and storage space in your kitchen by discarding the following: expired food and old spices, storage containers that are missing lids, chipped dishes and mugs, cookbooks, and aprons that you never use.

151 USE A STICKY NOTE

Decanting pantry staples such as flour, sugar, rice, and pasta into clear air-tight storage containers is a good way to keep them organized and pest free, but then you lose valuable packaging information. Stick a note on the back of the container with the expiration date and cooking instructions.

152 SEND ANTS PACKING

If ants have invaded, the first step is determining what's attracting them. Standing water and sugar are the two biggest culprits, so inspect your pantry and cabinets for drips and spills. Next, clean their path—or wherever you're noticing them—really well with the Nonabrasive Vinegar Cleaner (see tip 076). Finally, repel them naturally by spraying your windowsills and doorways with a mixture of water and essential oils (peppermint and lavender are two scents ants despise). If the infestation is bad, you'll have to step up your game. Boric acid is an effective ant killer. Make a DIY bait by combining some boric acid in a dish with jelly. The ants will carry the poison back to their colony and destroy them at the source.

153 CLEAN OUT THE CABINETS

Kitchen cabinets accumulate a layer of grime from the grease and steam in everyday cooking, but a quick wipe with warm soapy water once a week will keep it from getting noticeably thick. Tackle the spills and drips when they happen. Make it a habit to do a daily spot check to look for a spill that you may have missed. Every 6 months, empty the cabinets and do an all-out sweep of the interior shelves where crumbs and minor spills have escaped your attention.

CREATE SPACE

If you weren't blessed with a plethora of cabinetry, add extra storage by bringing in a baker's rack, stacking dishes on wall shelves, hanging a magnetic knife rack, or utilizing a pot rack. Because these open areas will be more exposed to grease, steam, and dust, be sure to stock them with your most frequently used items that will naturally be washed often.

QUICK TIP

STERILIZE YOUR SPONGE

Your sponge may get so dirty that rinsing is not enough. Add it to the top rack of your dishwasher for your next load. Squeeze out excess water and microwave it for four minutes, and the heat will kill most of the bacteria.

ORGANIZE YOUR JUNK DRAWER

The toss-it-in-and-forget-about-it nature of a junk drawer is what makes it so appealing—until you spend 15 minutes hunting for your tape measure, spare key, or gift card you're finally ready to use. Because a junk drawer needs to hold so many random things, it's difficult to keep it organized by item like you may in other areas. An easy way to add a little more order to the chaos is by putting in an expandable utensil drawer tray. A single organizer works better than a mishmash of smaller boxes and cups because it doesn't slide around or tip. The scissors still may end up with the pens, but at least everything's not swirling around together.

MOVE COUPONS OUT OF THE HOUSE

Instead of sticking clipped coupons to the fridge or shoving them in a folder never to be seen again, put them in a small pouch in your purse, glove box, or backpack. This way, when you're out and about, you'll have easy access to them. Whenever you're stuck killing time, like in a waiting room, riding the subway, or driving through the car wash, take a couple minutes to sort through your coupons and toss any that have expired.

FIND A NEW HOME FOR YOUR CUTLERY

Tight on space? Instead of letting your forks and spoons take up valuable drawer space, move them to your dining table. There are loads of adorable tabletop utensil holders to fit every style, or just keep it simple with a few upcycled jars or cans.

BRIGHTEN CABINET DOORS

Cabinets with natural and painted wood, laminate, and stainless steel doors need only a few minutes of your attention to keep them looking beautiful. Just remember to avoid any abrasive sponges, scrubbers, or cleaning products, which will scratch and dull the finish.

STEP ONE Mist a solution of castile soap and warm water on a microfiber cloth and wipe the cabinet and drawer panels.

STEP TWO Wipe again with a clean damp cloth to remove the soap, and once again with a clean dry cloth.

STEP THREE Inspect the hinges and hardware connections, and use a toothbrush to dislodge grime that you find.

159 CLEAN BEHIND CLOSED DOORS

Hidden spaces on the inside of cabinets, drawers, and the pantry can often get overlooked in between cooking and family life. The worst cases are often the junk drawer and the space under the sink, but all interior spaces need a seasonal cleaning to avoid crud creep. There's no better time to declutter, tossing seldom-used utensils, matchbooks, and overflowing rubber bands. If you just can't part with the special-occasion utensils or little-used pots and pans, move them to a shelf or drawer on the edge of your work area.

EXPOSE Throw open all the doors and cabinets and empty them—grouping the contents in the order you intend to restore them—and stash them in bins.

CLEANSE Take the time to thoroughly vacuum all interior spaces with the dust-brush attachment, then wipe with a soft cloth or sponge dampened with the All-Purpose Cleaner (see tip 076).

EXCAVATE Scrub the edges and cracks with a toothbrush before wiping away the cleaner with a cloth dampened with water only.

SHINE While they're out, wipe all utensils with the Nonabrasive Vinegar Cleaner (see tip 076).

REPLACE Let drawers and shelves dry completely before returning the contents. Use the same process to clean pantry shelves.

160 USE A LINER

Shelf liners can be a solution for several kitchen conundrums. If you're dealing with a specific cleaning or organization headache, see if a liner might help.

GRIPPY LINER Keeps fragile dinnerware from shifting, and they wipe clean.

WASHABLE LINER Makes cleaning up fridge spills a breeze.

ADHESIVE-FREE LINER Protects painted shelves from getting chipped or scuffed.

WIRE-SHELF LINER An answer for wire pantry shelves and kitchen racks.

161 DON'T LET SPILLS LINGER

It's important to keep the shelves of your cabinets clean, otherwise an unattended mess will transfer to every jar, box, can, and bottle that you store. Often, the type of spill will determine the best course of action.

GREASY Use the Nonabrasive Vinegar Solution (see tip 076). Vinegar cuts through grease, making it easy to remove with a microfiber cloth. You may need to make two passes, as your first wiping may lift off most of the loosened grease, but spread the remainder.

STICKY For peanut butter or honey drips, fill a plastic bag with ice and hold it on the spill until it hardens. Then gently scrape it off with the bowl of a plastic spoon.

COLORFUL If there are spots of juice or wine stains that don't come off, generously sprinkle baking soda on a barely damp sponge and hold it over the spot, repeating as needed. Rinse to remove all traces of baking soda and dry the spot.

162 GET A HANDLE ON IT

Cabinet and drawer handles are the primary point of human contact, so they're continually exposed to the dirt and oils of your hands. They're also easy to overlook, since it's specifically the inside of a door pull or knob that's handled.

Wash knobs and handles with hot, soapy water and a soft cloth, then dry and buff with another cloth. During the winter months, when colds spread through the family, spray them with the Disinfectant (see tip 076) to decrease the chance of lingering germs.

CHECKLISTS

The challenge of thinking, "I'll just wash this dish later," is how that one dish quickly turns into two dishes … and four bowls, and three drinking glasses, and a scattering of utensils! Take care of those dirty dishes, stovetop drips, and other small cleanups before they snowball into bigger messes. Numbers refer to the general cleaning tips, so make sure to reference the appropriate supporting tips to address specific materials and circumstances.

DAILY
- ☐ Sweep or vacuum floors 039
- ☐ Wipe counters and tables 131
- ☐ Wipe stovetop 101
- ☐ Wash dishes 107
- ☐ Load and run dishwasher 115
- ☐ Wipe dishwasher exterior 114
- ☐ Clean sink 123
- ☐ Wipe faucets 128
- ☐ Clean minor appliances 100, 140, 141, 145, 146, 147
- ☐ Put out new dish towels 084

WEEKLY
- ☐ Dust window treatments 019
- ☐ Dust doors and baseboards 023
- ☐ Clean switch plates 024
- ☐ Dust ceilings and walls 026
- ☐ Mop floors 040
- ☐ Dust lampshades and chandeliers 065, 069
- ☐ Clean refrigerator interior and exterior 086
- ☐ Clean stovetop 101
- ☐ Clean disposal 125
- ☐ Wipe cabinet doors 158
- ☐ Disinfect handles and knobs 162

MONTHLY
- ☐ Clean window treatments 019
- ☐ Wash trash cans 037
- ☐ Clean doorknobs 038
- ☐ Steam clean microwave 100
- ☐ Sanitize dishwasher interior 119
- ☐ Deep clean disposal 125
- ☐ Deep clean minor appliances 100, 140, 141, 145, 146, 147
- ☐ Clean knobs 162

SEASONALLY (SPRING AND FALL)
- ☐ Wash windows 017
- ☐ Deep clean window treatments 019
- ☐ Wipe doors and baseboards 023
- ☐ Clean walls 026
- ☐ Clean light fixtures, chandeliers, and sconces 067, 069, 070
- ☐ Deep clean refrigerator and freezer 086
- ☐ Replace liners 160
- ☐ Clean condenser coils 091
- ☐ Deep clean stove and oven 096
- ☐ Clean vent hood and filter 106
- ☐ Deep clean dishwasher and filter 120
- ☐ Scour disposal 126
- ☐ Clean knife block 143
- ☐ Clean out cabinets and pantry 153
- ☐ Clean inside cabinets and drawers 153
- ☐ Reseal countertops 131

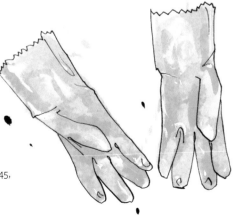

163 START THE DAY RIGHT

A clean and uncluttered bathroom gives the day an energizing kick start. Designate a quick 5 minutes to the bathroom-tidying items below every evening before bed and every morning after you're ready for the day. It's cathartic, a symbolic taking control of your space that propels you through the rest of your day.

- Quickly wipe down faucets, sinks, and counters.
- Swish the toilets
- Clean the shower as you finish, using a squeegee to wipe away soap scum and water minerals.

164 USE A COLOR CODE

Microfiber cloths absorb more than a soft cloth, rag, or sponge, but use a different cloth for general cleaning than for cleaning the toilet. Buy one of a different color for the toilet so you're less likely to confuse them. Also keep a second pair of rubber gloves in the same color as your designated toilet microfiber cloth. Microfiber cloths used in the bath don't rest in the laundry hamper with clothes; they go directly into the washer in a load by themselves.

165 STOCK A BATH CADDY

If cleaners are within easy reach, you're more apt to use them daily. Store the shower cleaner on the rack with soap and shampoo. Stash other supplies beneath the sink or in nearby cabinets. If there's no extra space behind closed doors, organize supplies in a stylish wicker basket or metal caddy. If you prefer a basket, pick one with sides just higher than the tallest bottle to shield supplies. Your bath caddy should include:

- All-Purpose Cleaner (see tip 076)
- Disinfectant (see tip 170)
- Glass Cleaner (see tip 014)
- Nonabrasive Vinegar Cleaner (see tip 170)
- Rubber gloves for general cleaning.
- Rubber gloves in another color for toilet cleaning
- Toilet Bowl Bombs (see tip 170)
- Tub 'n' Tile Cleaner (see tip 170)

166 BE COURTEOUS

Whether you're sharing a bathroom with family or roommates, boundaries and thoughtfulness go a long way toward maintaining a happy relationship. Try to always do the following: Clear hair from the drain after showering or bathing; change the toilet paper roll when it's empty; and close the toilet lid after using it. If these manners aren't being reciprocated, an honest conversation is always better than seething with resentment.

167
RELOCATE

If there's only one bathroom (or just not enough bathrooms for the number of people in your household), think about which grooming routines could be moved elsewhere. Setting up a vanity or good mirror near a window and outlet could allow you to apply makeup and style your hair in your bedroom.

168
STORE TOYS

Gather bath toys in a mesh bag or bath storage basket in the tub. Choosing something that will allow excess water to drain will keep mildew at bay.

169
GO HIGH

In a small bathroom, consider how you can maximize your vertical space. Wall shelves are handy for keeping essentials such as spare toilet paper close at hand and for displaying décor or artwork.

MAKE BATHROOM CLEANSERS

With a little TLC, your bathroom can be an oasis in your home. Use these natural cleaning products to help disinfect, deodorize, and cut through any soapy buildup.

NOTE: Remember that while natural cleaners can be useful for cleaning and getting that sparkle and shine, they don't quite cut it for sanitizing germy surfaces. For that, turn to an all-purpose cleaner. There are several plant-based disinfectants that are effective at killing bacteria and viruses.

DISINFECTANT

2 tbsp. liquid castile soap
20 drops tea tree oil

Mix the soap and essential oil with hot water in a 16-oz. spray bottle.

TOILET BOWL BOMBS

1 $\frac{1}{2}$ c. baking soda
$\frac{1}{2}$ c. citric acid powder
20 drops peppermint essential oil

Thoroughly mix the baking soda and citric acid powder in a bowl. Slowly stir in the peppermint essential oil to evenly distribute. Use a spray bottle to sparingly mist water into the mixture—stirring to uniformly moisten the powder—until the powder sticks together in clumps. The mixture will slightly fizz from the moisture, so make sure not to oversaturate.

Firmly pack a silicone mold with the moist mixture and leave out to dry overnight, wiping off any excess from the fizzing. Gently remove the formed bomb from the mold and store in a sealable container. Add a finished bomb to the toilet bowl and allow to fizz. Once the bomb has dissolved, flush out the bowl water.

NONABRASIVE VINEGAR CLEANER

1 part distilled white vinegar
2 parts water
5 drops essential oil

Combine the vinegar and water in a 16-oz. spray bottle. Add 5 drops of essential oil such as lavender, grapefruit, orange, lemon, or peppermint if you don't like the smell of vinegar.

TOILET BOWL CLEANER

liquid castile soap
$\frac{1}{2}$ c. baking soda

Squirt the liquid castile soap under the rim of the toilet bowl, then sprinkle the baking soda into the bowl. Scrub with a toilet brush, and flush to rinse.

TUB 'N' TILE CLEANER

$\frac{1}{2}$ c. borax
$\frac{1}{2}$ c. baking soda
1 tsp. liquid castile soap
2–3 c. hot water

Thoroughly mix all ingredients in a bucket.

GROUT CLEANER

$\frac{3}{4}$ c. baking soda
$\frac{1}{2}$ c. hydrogen peroxide
2–3 c. water

Mix all ingredients into a paste, apply to the grout, and let sit for 15 minutes. Scrub with a grout brush or toothbrush, staying within the grout lines.

171 KEEP IT FRESH

Given damp towels, dirty clothes, and regular use, the bathroom can deliver daily olfactory assaults. Implement a few steps to keep it smelling as clean as it looks. Turn on the vent when you enter the bath to help remove both excess moisture and bacteria in the air. Open a window whenever possible to allow the moisture to dissipate.

ABSORB Fill a cute bowl with baking soda to absorb odors.

CONTAIN Invest in a lidded wastebasket and empty it often.

FRESHEN Keep a fresh arrangement of sweet-smelling flowers in a vase or light a scented candle when you have guests in the house.

RELEASE Add some drops of essential oil onto the side of a toilet paper roll. Each time you unroll it, the aroma will be released into the air.

172
TRANSFER SOAP TO PRETTY PUMP BOTTLES

Buying your shampoo, conditioner, and body wash in bulk is the most economical choice. However, these giant bottles often don't fit in your shower caddy or niche. Having them cluttering up your floor is no good either. Instead, transfer the soap into smaller, refillable pump bottles that fit your aesthetic. Bonus: When neatly lined up, the matching bottles look positively spa-like.

173
PICK A PUMP

If you prefer a pump-style soap dispenser, it's less expensive and wasteful to choose a refillable style than disposable plastic soap pump bottles. Cleaning a glass soap dispenser is pretty straightforward. Whenever it's running empty, don't just pour more soap on top of whatever's stuck in the bottom. Instead, add a little warm water and a few drops of vinegar, then give it a few squirts to clear out the pump. Unscrew the top, and wash the bottle in the dishwasher. When it's clean and dry, it's ready for a refill!

174

ORGANIZE YOUR MEDICINE CABINET

The bathroom medicine cabinet is one of those places that collects clutter and develops a layer of grime from humidity and dust. Follow these steps to keep it just as fresh as the rest of your bathroom.

EMPTY Pull everything out of the cabinet and throw out anything you won't use including little foil sample packets of lotion, perfume and cologne, and beauty products. If you haven't used it in a year, you probably never will!

STERILIZE Spray the interior of the cabinet with the Disinfectant (see tip 170) and wipe all shelves and crevices. If you have removable glass shelves, take them out and clean with the Glass Cleaner (see tip 014).

RESTOCK Add back the things you'll actually use, including the little containers of supplies that would otherwise clutter your counter. Anything you regularly use and are likely to replace within 3 to 6 months will not be around long enough to be harmed by the humidity in the bath. Deodorant, toothpaste, shaving cream, and skin creams are all good candidates.

175 STORE YOUR MEDICINES SAFELY

The bathroom cabinet is not the best place to store medications because steam from the shower and bath can alter their effectiveness. Pull everything out and check expiration dates, then toss those with expired dates. (Don't flush medicines down the toilet—call your pharmacy to find out where you can locally dispose of the medications.) Move over-the-counter medications, vitamins, and prescription drugs to a cool, dry place out of the reach of children and teens.

176 KEEP MINIS

Have a basket in your bathroom for travel-sized toiletries you buy or bring home from hotels. When it's time to travel, just grab and go. They're also convenient for overnight guests to help themselves to.

QUICK TIP

TIDY JARS AND BOTTLES

Simplify your routine by designating a shelf in your medicine cabinet for your skin care routine. Arrange the products in the order you use them, then just work your way through the lineup.

177 GET CREATIVE

Try hanging a shoe organizer on the back of your bathroom door to minimize clutter. It has lots of pockets for bottles, brushes, and hair tools. For a crowded household, you could even designate one row of pockets for each family member or roommate.

178

REMEMBER
BATHROOM RECYCLING

It's too easy to toss your empties in your bathroom trash can. Try placing a shoebox in your bathroom closet or under the sink to collect the following recyclables:

- Shampoo, conditioner, body wash, and lotion bottles
- Cardboard boxes from toothpaste or medicine packaging
- Toilet-roll tubes
- Deodorant tubes
- Shaving-foam bottles
- Hand-soap bottles (ditch the pump)

QUICK TIP

TOSS THE JUNK

As you're organizing, take the opportunity to throw away bottles of dried-up nail polish, stretched-out hair ties, and products you tried and didn't like.

179

TAKE CARE WITH
PILL BOTTLES

Although most plastic prescription bottles are made of recyclable plastic, their small size often makes them slip through the curbside recycling screening process . Your local pharmacy may have a drop-off recycling program. Another option is to save them and repurpose them as travel-sized containers for earbuds, jewelry, bobby pins, Q-tips, a sewing kit, or toiletries (when flying, use bottles that are 3.4 ounces or less for liquids).

180 MAKE YOUR SHOWER SPARKLE

It may seem odd that a space that gets a daily dose of soap and water needs cleaning daily, but soap leaves scum and water leaves spots. It takes just a couple of minutes to avoid the time-consuming task of removing a thick layer of soap buildup. Scrub the shower walls, door, and tracks each week to remove mineral deposits.

SQUEEGEE EVERY DAY Before you leave the shower, spray the walls and doors with the Nonabrasive Vinegar Cleaner (see tip 170) or a cleaner appropriate to the wall material (see "A Cautionary Tale" below), and use the squeegee to remove soap along with the cleaning solution. Follow the squeegee with a microfiber-cloth wipe, much like you wipe your windshield with paper towels after using the squeegee on it.

A CAUTIONARY TALE Vinegar is harmful to stone tile such as slate, marble, granite, and travertine. Composite granite and quartz, as well as cultured marble, should also not be cleaned with vinegar. Use a solution of soap and water, squeegee, and dry.

SHOWER CURTAINS Liners and curtains can be washed with a mild detergent in cold water on the gentle cycle of a front-load washer, with $1/2$ c. white vinegar in the machine's fabric-softener dispenser. Be cautious with a top-load washer—the agitator can damage the curtain with direct contact. Try adding a barrier of rags around the agitator, or spot-clean with the Nonabrasive Vinegar Cleaner and thoroughly rinse.

181 DEGUNK SHOWER TRACKS

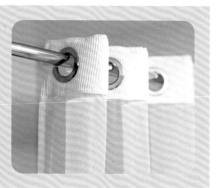

Shower tracks are a hot spot for filth. Sometimes even a good scrubbing needs a little extra help. One way to give it a boost is to soak strips of paper towel in white vinegar, and then nestle them into the tracks of the shower door. Let the vinegar do its thing for about 30 minutes, and then throw the strips away. Use a brush to scrub away any remaining scum.

182 WAVE A WAND

Stay on top of cleaning your shower by stashing a refillable brush wand—the same kind you may use for dishes—inside your shower. Depending on whether your primary struggle is soap scum or grime, fill it with either white vinegar or dish soap, and swipe the shower walls and door while you're getting yourself clean. Don't forget to rinse off whatever you clean. A removable shower head makes spraying everything down quick and easy.

183 CLEAN YOUR SHOWERHEAD

Minerals can build up within the showerhead and impede the fast and straight flow of water, but cleaning the head is pretty easy if you just follow these steps:

STEP ONE Use a toothbrush or grout brush to scrub the showerhead once a month.

STEP TWO Every three months, fill a plastic bag with white distilled vinegar and tie the bag around the showerhead so the head is submerged in the vinegar.

STEP THREE Let the bag sit overnight, and the vinegar will dissolve the mineral buildup.

STEP FOUR Remove the bag and scrub the head with a toothbrush or microfiber cloth.

STEP FIVE Turn on the shower full blast to clear the showerhead.

AIR IT OUT

Having an operational vent is key to removing excess moisture from the bathroom and is a preventative step to discourage mildew. But it works most efficiently if it's clean. At least twice a year, perform the following maintenance:

DISENGAGE Turn off the electricity to the bathroom.

REMOVE Secure a ladder beneath the vent and remove the vent cover. (Be prepared for dust and gunk to fall out.)

SOAK Submerge the vent cover in warm, soapy water.

VACUUM With a handheld mini-vac or a dust-brush attachment, vacuum the fan blades.

WIPE Dampen a microfiber cloth in warm, soapy water and wipe down each fan blade. You may need a toothbrush to clean otherwise inaccessible spots.

DRY Make sure the vent cover is dry before replacing it.

185 GO AFTER GROUT

Stone and high-gloss ceramic tiles can be dulled by vinegar and lemon juice, so apply the Grout Cleaner (see tip 170). Leave it for 15 minutes and then scrub with a grout brush, keeping within the lines. Rinse all traces away with warm water.

186 KEEP CAULK CLEAN

Whenever you're scrubbing the grout in your bathroom, you should also clean the caulk. Besides keeping it free from dirt and hair, regular cleaning will also keep it from growing bacteria, mold, or mildew. A mixture of water and hydrogen peroxide will do the trick. If you notice your caulk is drying, cracking, or peeling, it's best to replace it sooner rather than later to prevent water damage.

QUICK TIP

PASS THE BAR

Soap scum results from the talc in bar soap. You'll have less soap scum if you opt for liquid body wash or glycerin soap.

KNOW YOUR BATHTUB

Whether it's the site of a nightly calming experience (think essential oils, soy candles, and bubbles) or a parental necessity (baby shampoo, rubber ducks, and bubbles), the bathtub needs to be clean and inviting. Here are dependable cleaning approaches tailored to the bathtub material of your home, with cleaning recipes you can find in tip 170. And remember to periodically use the Disinfectant to sanitize your tub.

MATERIAL	CLEANING METHOD	TIPS & TRICKS	AVOID
ACRYLIC	Clean with mild soap and water. Rinse well. Dry to prevent water spotting.	Use a soft cloth and elbow grease on tough spots. Step up to the Nonabrasive Vinegar Cleaner if necessary.	Abrasive sponges and cleaners will scratch the surface.
COPPER AND NICKEL	Rinse well and dry after each use. Weekly, wash with mild soap and water. Rinse well and dry.	Copper and nickel with a protective coating need only rinsing and a quick wipe.	Abrasives will scratch. Acidic cleaning products will pit copper.
CULTURED MARBLE, COMPOSITE GRANITE, ONYX, AND QUARTZ	Use only mild soap and a soft cloth. Rinse well and dry after every use.	Reseal the tub annually to diminish staining.	Avoid scouring pads and abrasive cleaning products, ammonia-based products, and bleach.
FIBERGLASS	Rinse and dry after every use. In hardwater areas, spray after every use with the Nonabrasive Vinegar Cleaner, rinse, and dry.	Attack resistant stains with a baking soda paste.	Abrasive sponges and cleaners will scratch. Toys and bottles left in or on the tub can stain.
MARBLE	Clean with mild soap and water after every use. Dry thoroughly.	Bath oils, shampoos, body washes, and shaving creams can discolor marble. Reseal annually to maintain stain resistance.	Never use abrasive or acidic materials.
PORCELAIN ENAMEL OVER CAST IRON OR STEEL	Clean with mild soap and water. Rinse and dry. For deeper cleaning, use the Tub 'n' Tile Cleaner.	For stains, dip half a lemon cut side down in baking soda and use it to scrub. Rinse and dry.	Avoid caustic chemical cleaning products.
SOLID SURFACE	Clean with warm, soapy water and a sponge. Rinse and dry.	For stains, use a nonabrasive scrubber with baking soda or vinegar.	Water that dries on the surface creates an unsightly film. Dry often.

188 TREAT YOUR TUB RIGHT

Freestanding tubs in which the tub's interior may be sheathed in a different material than its interior are increasingly common, such as a porcelain interior with a stainless exterior, or a nickel interior with a copper exterior. Follow the recommendations in tip 187 for cleaning specific materials, however they may be used. More common are built-in tub surrounds of wood, tile, or stone that support a drop-in tub. When cleaning, treat these materials as you would a wall (see tips 030–033) or countertop (see tips 131–132).

189 EXTEND YOUR REACH

If it's difficult for you to clean your tub and tile on your hands and knees, try a scrubber with an extendable handle. It's a total game changer for folks with mobility challenges.

190 SANITIZE THE WHIRLPOOL

A relaxing luxury, a whirlpool tub requires thorough, regular cleaning to halt the growth of bacteria and mold. After each use, rinse it well and dry with a towel to eliminate lingering moisture. Because they are easily molded, acrylic and fiberglass whirlpools are common, but check tip 187 for cleaning practices for your specific tub body. When possible, read and follow manufacturer's instructions because many whirlpools have piping and jet designs that require specialized cleaning techniques. At least once a month, clean and disinfect your whirlpool by following these simple steps:

STEP ONE Fill the tub with enough water to reach around 3 in. above the jets and then add 1 c. white vinegar and 2 tbsp. of a mild liquid soap.

STEP TWO Turn the whirlpool on for 15 minutes.

STEP THREE Drain the tub and refill again to 3 in. above the jets. This time, run the jets for 10 minutes before draining.

STEP FOUR Clean the individual jets by dipping a toothbrush in vinegar and scrubbing the holes. Rinse the toothbrush in water and rub within the holes to rinse away all gunk.

191 CLEAR DRAINS NATURALLY

Hair and soap scum readily clog bathroom drains, but fortunately it's easy to get the water moving again without resorting to acidic chemical dissolvers. Commercial drain cleaners are highly toxic and will damage many sink, tub, and shower materials if you accidentally spill as you pour the solutions into the drain. Instead, try this method to dislodge clogs without the acrid smell and potential for damage.

BOIL Start an electric kettle with 2–3 qt. water, or bring to a boil in a large kettle on the stovetop.

COMBINE Mix 1 c. table salt and 1 c. baking soda and pour it down the drain.

BUBBLE Slowly pour 1 c. vinegar into the drain and let it bubble for 1–2 minutes.

PURGE Clear the drain by pouring in the boiling water. Wipe the drain cover with a soft cloth to make sure no salt or vinegar remains.

Repeat these steps monthly and your pipes will stay clear and you'll increase the probability that you can avoid serious trouble and costly calls to a professional plumber.

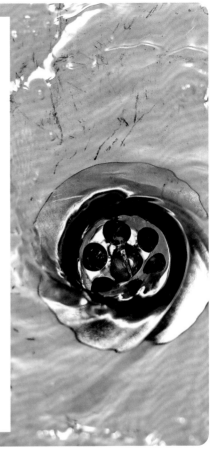

192

PULL HAIR FROM YOUR DRAIN

If you haven't been keeping up on clearing your drains, you may have a hair clog that needs a bit more muscle to remove. A drain stick or a drain snake is just what it sounds like: a long, skinny rod that you push down the drain. Turn the handle until it grabs hold of the grossness so you can pull it out.

193 TAKE CARE OF YOUR TOWELS

We all love the scent of freshly laundered towels after an invigorating shower, so make sure every towel in your house gets washed regularly. You don't need to wash them every day because there's limited time, washing wears out the towel, and it's not environmentally responsible. If you take care of your towels, you only need to wash them after every three or four uses.

OWN Do not share towels among family members. Everyone should have their own hook or rack for hanging their towel until it's time for the weekly wash. A towel bar allows quicker air-drying than a hook.

DEHUMIDIFY Turn on the vent or open a window so that air circulates during and after the shower. It minimizes the moisture in the air, making the towels less hospitable to the growth of bacteria.

SMELL Be wary of stinky towels. When you smell moldy towels, wash them on the hottest setting, take them from the washer immediately after the cycle finishes, and put them in the dryer.

194

SHOP SMART

Thick towels require extra time and energy to dry and take up more storage space. For a more energy- and space-efficient option, make the switch to Turkish towels or quick-dry bath towels that often contain microfiber. It may sound counterintuitive, but often these lightweight versions are more absorbent than super-plush towels.

195 REMEMBER THE ROBE

Terry bathrobes can provide a degree of luxury to your postbath experience if they're soft, fluffy, and clean. As with towels, the challenge is to keep them fresh in a humid environment, especially when absorbing excess moisture from your body after a hot shower. But robes have an additional challenge: You may feel clean after that shower, but skin cells rub off onto the robe as you wear it. These cells build up and are vulnerable to bacteria growth and its accompanying smells.

To keep your terry bathrobe fresh, let it air out and thoroughly dry after each use. Bathrobes are similar to bath towels in that they won't dry well if left in a clump on the floor. It takes just a few seconds to hang your robe from a hook; if you don't have a designated place to keep your robe, make one. Adding another piece of bathroom hardware to the wall is simple enough for anyone to do and will go a long way toward keeping your house tidy.

Wash your robe every time you wash your towels to maintain a hygienic routine and tumble dry on low heat to fluff up the terry loops, which get matted down during the washing machine's spin cycle. As with all textiles, consult the labels for specific care instructions, especially with silk and linen.

196 LAUNDER ALL BATH MATS

Fabric bath mats hold onto moisture and mold through repeated contact with wet feet and the bathroom floor, so wash them at least once a week. Even with a rubber backing, a mat can be machine-washed on a warm or cold setting. A rubber backing will fare better if the mat is hung outside to dry, away from direct sunlight. If your bath mat does not have a rubber backing, machine-wash in hot water and then move it into the dryer. Similarly, contour bath mats that fit around your toilet should be washed as directed above and dried according to whether they have a rubber backing.

QUICK TIP

PICK IT UP

A bath mat is different than an area rug. When it's not in use, drape it over the side of your bathtub.

CLEAN SINKS AND VANITY TOPS

Sinks and vanity tops are available in a dazzling assortment of materials and colors, and while a few materials have specific requirements for care, most are best cleaned with just a little soap and water. Cleaning and drying after every use are critical, however, to diminish water spotting. Clean as you go or work harder later.

Spread a mild liquid soap mixed with warm water on both the sink and the vanity counter, wiping with a sponge or microfiber cloth, then dry with another cloth. If you prefer something stronger, clean with the Disinfectant (see tip 170).

FIRST, DO NO HARM

Whenever feasible, refer to the manufacturer's instructions for cleaning your particular sink material. Follow the guidelines below to keep these areas spotlessly clean while minimizing the risk of stains or discoloration.

WIPE Quickly wipe up toothpaste, lotions, and makeup, as they can stain.

DRY Rinse and dry with a towel after every use. While it may seem silly to dry a sink, it effectively diminishes water spotting.

AVOID Abrasive cleaning pads and commercial cleaners can scratch delicate surfaces, and bleach and ammonia-based cleaners can chemically damage surfaces.

PROTECT If commercial drain cleaners get on the surrounding sink, they can damage it. See tip 191 for how to unclog your drain using all-natural materials.

199 TREAT STAINS ON PORCELAIN

A material often used for sinks, but rarely for countertops, is porcelain enamel. For stains on porcelain enamel sinks as well as tubs, dip $1/2$ lemon, cut side down, in baking soda and use it to scrub the stain. Rinse well and dry.

200 DECLUTTER DRAWERS AND CABINETS

All the nooks and crannies need to be seasonally cleaned and decluttered. Empty the drawers and cabinets so you can thoroughly vacuum all interior spaces with a dust-brush attachment. Then wipe with a soft cloth or sponge dampened with the All-Purpose Cleaner (see tip 076). Use a toothbrush to clean the edges and corners. Wipe again with a cloth dampened with water to remove any trace of the cleaner. Let them dry completely before replacing the contents.

QUICK TIP

STAY FILM FREE

After giving your countertops a thorough cleaning, instead of air-drying them, be sure to wipe them completely dry to avoid a buildup of film on the surface.

201 THINK ABOUT ACCESS

Keep kid-safe bathroom items such as spare toiletries and Band-Aids on the bottom shelves of your vanity or bath closet so they can help themselves. Keep things that require grown-up supervision out of reach.

202 KEEP A MAKEUP DRAWER PRETTY

A pinch of face powder, a sprinkle of eye shadow, and a drop of foundation all accumulate in the makeup drawer, in spite of our best efforts.

Remove everything, discarding old makeup and all those free samples you thought you'd try and never did. Makeup doesn't usually have a printed expiration date, although the rule of thumb for mascara is 6 months. Adopt that time period and toss things that have gone unused since then.

Rejuvenate the drawer itself by following the process in tip 200. Wash all organizers and clean cosmetic bottles and tubes before returning them to the drawer. (Toss if they are a lost cause.)

203 TREASURE YOUR JEWELRY

Jewelry boxes and trays lined with velvet, felt, or fabric collect dust, and you'll be caught in a never-ending cycle of cleaning your jewelry unless you clean up their home. Follow these steps to keep your jewelry shining bright:

STEP ONE Close or cover your sink drain so you don't lose a favorite earring, then lay out a towel to protect both the counter and your jewelry as you empty the box or drawer.

STEP TWO Remove any drawer organizers or trays and clean the drawer (see tip 202).

STEP THREE Use cotton swabs—dampened if needed—to get the dirt out of the cushioned compartment for rings and out of corners. Wipe all the fabric-lined surfaces with a barely damp microfiber cloth.

STEP FOUR For more cleaning power, vacuum with a dust-brush attachment or use compressed air to dislodge dust.

204 WIPE DOWN BATH FIXTURES

A quick wipedown daily will keep your bath fixtures looking like new. Most faucets and handles, shower hardware, and towel bars installed within the last 20 years have a factory-applied coating that is stain and tarnish resistant. You need only wipe the hardware with a soft cloth after every use to remove fingerprints and water spotting. Be diligent, because minerals in the water and soap scum left to sit will wear away the protective coating over time.

205 GET IN CREVICES

To scrape gunk from the cracks around your faucet, sink edge, or vents, use a chopstick or toothpick that's wrapped with a cloth.

206 GIVE IT A SHINE

A natural way to polish your bathroom faucets is to add a couple of drops of olive oil on a cleaning cloth, then rub onto the faucets. You'll be amazed at how sparkly they get. If you try this with your bathtub or shower faucets, be careful to thoroughly clean up any dribbles of oil so you don't slip the next time you bathe.

 ## PRESERVE
COATINGS

Your overall goal with faucets and fixtures is to preserve their protective coating. If the applied coating is scratched or chipped, the base material is exposed to oxidization and can discolor. Stay away from abrasive cleaners and cleaning pads, bleach, ammonia, rubbing alcohol, acidic solutions, cleaning products designed to remove tarnish or rust, and polishes with harsh chemicals.

Many manufacturers use a process called physical vapor deposition (PVD) or a clean, protective-coated finish on fixtures of brass, copper, bronze, stainless, chrome, or nickel, so it may be impossible to identify whether an existing fixture is coated.

 ## CLEAN CLASSIC
HARDWARE

Fixtures over 20 years old are probably uncoated, though they can still be scratched by abrasive scrubbers, so rely only on soft cloths and sponges. Start with soapy water, rinse well, dry, and buff. If needed, step up to the Nonabrasive Vinegar Cleaner (see tip 170). Baking soda is a mild abrasive, and a baking soda paste is the next possibility for tough spots. Let it sit for 5 minutes, rinse with copious amounts of water to get rid of every trace of baking soda, dry, and buff.

LET A NATURAL PATINA DEVELOP

Uncoated brass, copper, and bronze, known as living finishes, are intended to change appearance over time. All of these are prized for the patina they develop with age and wear. Just keep water spots and soap scum off of them and avoid commercial cleaners and abrasive pads.

PLAY IT SAFE

If you can identify the faucet's manufacturer, check its website for specific cleaning instructions. If you're cleaning blind and want to remove accumulated water spots or soap, start with warm, soapy water, rinse well to remove all traces of soap, dry, and buff with a microfiber cloth. A soft toothbrush can dislodge dirt that may build up around the joints.

GO FOR THE GOLD

Some luxury faucets are plated in gold, which is a soft finish without protective coating. To safely clean gold plate, spray a vinegar-water solution (1 part vinegar to 3 parts water) on a soft cloth. Drape the cloth on the faucet or fixture and leave for 15 minutes. Gently rub with the wet cloth. Repeat if there is resistant dirt. Wipe with a water-soaked cloth, being sure to remove all of the vinegar-water solution. Dry with a fresh cloth.

272 CLEAN FAUCET HANDLES

Older bathroom faucet handles are often clear crystal or plastic and prone to calcium buildup or mildew. To get them clean, carefully pop off the end cap from the faucet handle with a flathead screwdriver. Next, remove the screw that holds the faucet handle on. Put the handle and the end cap in a bowl of vinegar for about 30 minutes. While they're soaking, use a microfiber cloth, toothbrush, and the Nonabrasive Vinegar Cleaner (see tip 170) to get rid of the scum. Then scrub the handle and the end cap. Rinse everything well and let it fully dry before putting it back together.

273 REJUVENATE MAKEUP BRUSHES

Dainty makeup brushes can collect enough goop to render them useless. Rather than throwing them away and replacing them, simply follow these directions to give your brushes a makeover.

RINSE Once a week, run barely warm tap water over the bristles of each brush without getting the handles wet.

LATHER Pour a few drops of mild liquid soap into your palm and massage the soap through the bristles. Rinse until the water runs clean, repeating as needed.

WRING With your fingers or a towel, gently squeeze excess water out of the brushes.

DRY Lay the brushes flat on a towel to dry. If you stand them with brush end up, the water will drain into the handle and loosen the bristles.

214 FRESHEN YOUR TOOTHBRUSH

The American Dental Association recommends a thorough rinsing of your toothbrush in warm water after brushing and letting the brush air-dry in an upright position. If you want more assurance, soak the brush in an antiseptic mouthwash for 15 minutes.

215 SCRUB CANISTERS, CUPS, AND DISHES

Tumblers for rinsing, canisters for cotton balls or toothbrushes, and soap dishes should take a run through the dishwasher once a week. If they aren't dishwasher safe, follow the guidelines for materials often found in sink and vanity tops (see tips 131–132). One problematic item is the soap dish, which often is gummed up with soap scum. Follow these steps to clean and maintain it for the future.

STEP ONE After emptying the soap dish, line it with a paste made from baking soda and water.

STEP TWO Let it sit for a few minutes, then scrub it with a toothbrush (or abrasive sponge if it won't scratch the finish), and rinse clean.

STEP THREE Once it's clean, put a little baby oil in the soap dish to make it easier to clean the next time.

216 TEND TO A HAIRBRUSH

Just as you have to wash your hair to remove dirt, oil, and built-up hair product, so too does your hairbrush need periodic cleaning to remove the same. As you follow these steps, remember to remove loose hairs that have accumulated in the sink to prevent future drain clogs.

STEP ONE Run a comb through your hairbrush until you can't get any more hair out of the bristles.

STEP TWO Fill the sink with warm water and a few drops of your favorite shampoo, and swish the brush in the water for a few minutes.

STEP THREE Run a comb through the brush again to remove loosened hair.

STEP FOUR Drain the sink and rinse the brush with warm water.

STEP FIVE Let the brush dry naturally on a towel, bristles down, so that all the water can drain out.

217 TAKE ON THE TOILET

We all probably agree that this our least favorite cleaning project, one that tempts us to procrastinate. For our family's health and our own peace of mind, however, it must be done—regularly.

DAILY Follow the recipe for the Toilet Bowl Cleaner (see tip 170), or toss in a couple of the Toilet Bowl Bombs (see tip 170) if you have unexpected company and you're pressed for time.

WEEKLY Flushing toilets scatters bacteria out of the bowl like a fountain, so the exterior needs a good weekly cleaning. Liberally spray with the Disinfectant (see tip 170) and wipe clean, starting with the tank top and working down to the base.

MONTHLY Turn the water off at the safety valve beneath the tank and flush to empty both the bowl and tank. Sprinkle baking soda around the inside of the bowl. Scrub the bowl and under the rim of the toilet to get rid of any dirt or stains. Pour 1 c. distilled vinegar around the inside of the bowl and let it sit for 1 hour.

Now it's time to clean the tank. Make a disinfectant spray of ¼ c. white vinegar to 1 c. water and spray on the walls of the empty tank. Start with a sponge or microfiber cloth to clean inside the tank and advance to a scrub brush and toothbrush if necessary to remove deposits. Turn on the water again and flush.

Calcium, magnesium, and other minerals in your water will accumulate on the bowl, and how often you need to remove them depends on your water's composition. In hard-water areas, plan to add this step when you have the water off and the bowl empty for monthly cleaning.

SOAK Fill the toilet bowl with distilled white vinegar and leave it overnight. Use a sponge soaked in vinegar to access under the rim.

SCOUR The next day, scrub the stains with your toilet brush or a stiff natural-bristle brush.

ADVANCE For resistant water rings and mineral stains, consider using a wet pumice stone, but only as a last resort. Applying too much pressure on the stone will damage the bowl.

RINSE Turn on the water and flush. You may need to repeat these steps to get rid of all deposits.

REMEMBER The best protection is to remove the deposits often so they don't build up over time.

QUICK TIP

REMOVE THE SEAT

Many modern toilet seats can be completely removed for a deep clean. They unlock and pop off so nothing can hide around the bolts.

219 CLEAN THE TOILET BRUSH

The toilet brush wins the prize for the dirtiest tool in the house. Clean it weekly by soaking the toilet brush in pure vinegar inside the brush holder. Pour enough vinegar to cover the brush, and leave it for several hours or overnight. After soaking, hold the brush over the toilet and pour the vinegar over it and into the bowl. Flush and rinse the brush in fresh water, and rinse the holder. Before returning the brush to its holder, put $1/4$ c. vinegar in the holder along with 10 drops tea tree oil. If you have pets, be sure to cover the solution.

220 CARE FOR SICK FAMILY MEMBERS

When someone becomes ill, assign them to a designated bedroom and, if possible, dedicate one bathroom for the patient's use only. If they are feeling up to being in the family room, label one chair or couch as only theirs for the duration.

221 QUARANTINE THE GERMS

If there is any time to be vigilant about general cleaning and especially cleaning the bathroom, it's when someone in your house gets sick. Speed healing, prevent contagion, and maintain some control by implementing a get-well-quick triage routine.

222 LAUNDER IN HOT WATER

Wash pillowcases, pajamas, hand towels, and—if practical—sheets every day. After the patient is feeling better, also wash blankets, duvet covers, and couch throws.

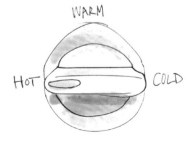

 WASH
YOUR HANDS

Washing with hand soap for 20 to 25 seconds is as critical as all other efforts to keep from spreading illness. During your routine, scrub your fingertips into your opposite palms or use a nailbrush to get germs hiding under your fingernails. Wash often and remind the rest of the household to do the same!

224 CONSIDER DISPOSABLES

Although minimizing waste and maximizing conservation efforts is always the best practice, this is a time when it makes sense to use paper towels and disposable wipes. Cloth wipes may, in fact, help spread germs and must be changed often.

QUICK TIP

SAVE ON WASTEBASKET CLEANING

A small garbage bag saves you the time of cleaning out the interior. Take a hint from hotel maids and leave a few bags folded at the bottom of the can so they are always handy. Once a month, clean the inside of the can with the Disinfectant (see tip 170).

STERILIZE SURFACES

At the end of the day, walk through the house with an eye toward anything the patient may have touched. Adhere to the directions and cautions specific to materials throughout this book, but follow these general guidelines. While vinegar and hydrogen peroxide are mild disinfectants, they do not kill all types of germs and bacteria. Follow up with hot, soapy water for maximum effectiveness. Clean doorknobs, light switches, cabinet handles, and the fridge door. Spray sinks and counters, toilets, and floors with the Nonabrasive Vinegar Cleaner (see tip 170) and then wash with hot, sudsy water.

DISINFECT EVERYTHING

After every use, wipe the thermometer with rubbing alcohol and let it air-dry before putting it away. Dip the patient's toothbrush in hydrogen peroxide and isolate it from other brushes. Dampen cotton pads with hydrogen peroxide and wipe frequently handled devices that may get overlooked such as:

- Cell phones and tablets
- Computer keyboards and mouses
- E-book readers
- Radio and stereo knobs
- Remote controls
- Video-game controllers

CHECKLISTS

Keeping the bathroom clean on a daily basis is much more efficient. Train your family to wipe down faucets, sinks, the shower, and the tub after every use. You can whisk through the rest in 5 minutes a day. Numbers refer to the general cleaning tips, so make sure to reference the appropriate supporting tips to address specific materials and circumstances.

DAILY
- ☐ Sweep or vacuum floors 039
- ☐ Wipe faucets 163
- ☐ Wipe sinks and counters 163
- ☐ Squeegee shower 163
- ☐ Rinse bathtub 163
- ☐ Rinse and dry whirlpool 163
- ☐ Swish toilets 217

WEEKLY
- ☐ Clean mirrors 018
- ☐ Dust window treatments 019
- ☐ Dust doors and baseboards 023
- ☐ Clean switch plates 024
- ☐ Dust ceilings and walls 026
- ☐ Mop floors 040
- ☐ Freshen air 171
- ☐ Scrub shower 180
- ☐ Deep clean tub 187
- ☐ Clean sink 197
- ☐ Wash towels, bath mats, and bathrobes 193, 195, 196
- ☐ Wash makeup and hairbrushes 213, 216
- ☐ Wash canisters, glasses, and soap dishes 215
- ☐ Wipe down toilet exterior and tank 217
- ☐ Clean toilet brush 219

MONTHLY
- ☐ Clean window treatments 019
- ☐ Wash trash cans 037
- ☐ Sanitize whirlpool tub 190
- ☐ Clear drains 191
- ☐ Clean tub exterior 188
- ☐ Deep clean toilet bowl and tank 217
- ☐ Remove minerals from toilet 218

SEASONALLY (SPRING AND FALL)
- ☐ Wash windows 017
- ☐ Deep clean window treatments 019
- ☐ Wipe doors and baseboards 023
- ☐ Clean walls 026
- ☐ Clean sconces and light fixtures 067, 070
- ☐ Restock bathroom caddy 165
- ☐ Purge medicine cabinet 174
- ☐ Wash shower curtain 180
- ☐ Clean showerhead 183
- ☐ Clean vent 184
- ☐ Clean grout 185
- ☐ Clean shelves, drawers, and cabinets 200
- ☐ Clean makeup drawer 202
- ☐ Clean jewelry box 203
- ☐ Restock bathroom caddy 165

227 DO LAUNDRY RIGHT

Few things are as satisfying as fresh, clean-smelling laundry neatly folded and then delivered to appropriate shelves, drawers, and closets. The trick is this: Don't let the clothes stack up. It really is as simple as that. As soon as you're up and dressed each morning, start one load of laundry and dry, fold, and put it away before day's end. Keep the laundry room clear with regular tidying and more in-depth attention to appliances every few months.

GET A JUMP START

Make setting up a load of laundry ready to go, complete with detergent, part of your evening routine. If your machine allows, set a delay start, or just simply have everything fixed so you can push the start button first thing in the morning.

MAINTAIN A FRESH HAMPER

Your hamper is like your garbage can; if it's storing dirty stuff, it needs to be cleaned, too! To start with, choose a hamper that has a removable fabric liner and/or is made of a woven material that provides some ventilation. About once a month, remove and launder the liner and wipe down the inside of the hamper with the Non-abrasive Vinegar Cleaner (see tip 239). Keep the lid open to dry and air out completely. (If you can put it outside in the sunshine, even better.) If you keep your hamper in the bathroom, this is also a good time to check for toothpaste smudges.

230

ORGANIZE THE LAUNDRY ROOM

Consolidating and purging clutter in the laundry room is the first step to maintaining a clean space. Organize cleaning supplies and related items in linen-lined baskets with labels. Use antique wire baskets or enamel trays to store laundry supplies. Once you organize your supplies, keeping it clean will be the easy part.

231

FIND A HOME FOR EVERYTHING

Your laundry room or mudroom are good spots for storing spare must-haves that otherwise don't seem to have a place to live. Like doorstops, outlet covers, felt furniture pads, and Command strips. Small, clear, stackable drawers will let you keep an eye on your stock.

 **FIND TEXTILE RECYCLING**

When clothes and linens are in such poor condition they can no longer be reused or donated, look into a textile recycling program. Many communities have designated days where you can drop off bags of these items so they can be cut into rags or repurposed as insulation or carpet padding.

 RECYCLE IN THE LAUNDRY ROOM

Keep a recycling can or paper bag in your laundry room to collect the following common recyclables:

- Detergent bottles and lids
- Plastic laundry powder or pod tubs and lids
- Dryer sheet boxes

NOTE: Most powdered laundry detergent boxes are coated in plastic and cannot be recycled.

 **GO HIGH**

Save space in your laundry room by hanging a wall-mounted drying rack. They easily pull down when you need them, and then fold right back up when your clothes are put away.

QUICK TIP

REPURPOSE LAUNDRY JUGS

Although they can be recycled, empty laundry detergent bottles have the ideal shape to be repurposed as watering cans. Clean the bottle well to remove any soap residue, and then carefully use a nail to poke holes in the cap. Fill it with water, screw on the cap, and then get watering your flowers.

235 SORT FOR YOU

Although in the past it was necessary, nowadays there's no rule that says you must sort darks from whites, brights, and so on. Modern washing machines and higher-quality fabrics make it very unlikely that colors will run if you wash in cold water. Think about what loads make the most sense for your home and family, and sort accordingly. Maybe each kid's clothes get washed all at once. Perhaps you need a load just for sweaty workout clothes. You may still choose to bleach white towels together and separate out a load of all denim, but if the system works for you, that's all that matters.

236 CLEAN THE COVER

Your ironing board cover provides a nice, flat (sometimes cushioned) surface for banishing wrinkles. But like everything else, it can accumulate its own dust and debris. Periodically remove it and give it a wash so this debris doesn't end up on your fresh clothes while you're ironing. Check the ironing board's care tag for instructions. Most recommend hand-washing (wipe with a damp sponge) or machine-washing (on a gentle cycle) and laying it flat to air-dry.

STEAM CLEAN
AN IRON

The flat metal base of the iron that becomes hot—known as the soleplate—can get gummed up with starch and mineral deposits. A similar buildup in the steam holes can decrease the iron's effectiveness and cause the iron to snag delicate blouses or shirts. Avoid this potentially costly problem by cleaning your iron at least once a year.

STEP ONE Set the heat to the highest setting (with the steam option disabled). Pour kosher or rock salt on top of a large paper bag and iron over the salt to dislodge anything stuck to the soleplate. Repeat with new salt until the soleplate is clean. Turn off the heat, let the iron cool, and wipe the soleplate.

STEP TWO Make a paste from 2 tbsp. baking soda and 1 tbsp. water, and spread it over the cold soleplate and into the steam holes. After a few minutes, wipe the soleplate clean with a damp microfiber cloth.

STEP THREE Use a cotton swab dampened with distilled water to clean out the steam holes. If they're still clogged from mineral deposits, dip the cotton swab in white vinegar and rub into the holes to dissolve mineral buildup.

STEP FOUR Fill the water reservoir with distilled water. Turn on the heat to the highest setting (with the steam option activated). When the iron is hot, press the steam button to flush out impurities.

If you live in a hard-water area, consider adding a mixture of $1/4$ c. white vinegar to $3/4$ c. distilled water into the reservoir for this process, but check the owner's manual to ensure you don't damage the iron.

STEP FIVE Turn off the iron and let it cool, then use a damp microfiber cloth to wipe away any debris that was pushed out by the steam, and empty the reservoir after cleaning.

238 REMOVE SCORCH MARKS

If you scorch an item while ironing it, you must act fast. Rub liquid laundry detergent into the stain, and then wash it right away. Unfortunately, heavily burned or melted areas are past the point of saving.

239 MAKE YOUR OWN SUPPLIES

The laundry room is a place to get clothes clean, but these products will help you keep your appliances clean, too. And with the simple homemade laundry detergent recipe below, you can forgo expensive retail detergents while maintaining their cleaning power!

NOTE: Remember that while natural cleaners can be useful for cleaning and getting that sparkle and shine, they don't quite cut it for sanitizing germy surfaces. For that, turn to an all-purpose cleaner. There are several plant-based disinfectants that are effective at killing bacteria and viruses.

ALL-PURPOSE CLEANER
2 tsp. borax
1/4 tsp. liquid castile soap
10 drops lemon essential oil

Mix all ingredients with hot water in a 16-oz. spray bottle.

NONABRASIVE VINEGAR CLEANER
1 part distilled white vinegar
2 parts water
5 drops essential oil

Combine the vinegar and water in a 16-oz spray bottle. Add 5 drops of essential oil such as lavender, grapefruit, orange, lemon, or peppermint if you don't like the smell of vinegar.

240 DEAL WITH TOUGH STAINS

Before you launch into treating a stain, remember these suggestions to make sure you do more good than harm.

KNOW Read the garment's care tag for specific instructions and cautions.

SAMPLE Test in an unnoticeable place in case your technique has adverse effects.

CHILL Always rinse and soak stains in cold water; warm or hot water can set the stain.

REFRAIN Never scrub stains; that may risk spreading the stain and fraying fibers.

ACCOMPLISH Remove the stain before laundering.

CONFIRM Air-dry after laundering to be certain the stain is gone.

PRESERVE Don't put the garment in the dryer until the stain is completely removed. Heat from a dryer or iron will set the stain permanently.

ENLIST Wool, silk, and other delicate fabrics and garments labeled "Dry Clean Only" should be turned over to a dry cleaner. Once you've worked on a stain unsuccessfully, the dry cleaner has less of a chance to get it out, so when in doubt, consult with a professional.

241 STOCK UP ON STAIN BUSTERS

You never know when a flick of mud or speckle of spaghetti sauce will strike, but any stain is easier to conquer while it is fresh. Be prepared so you can get a jump on accidents by creating a toolbox of stain-fighting products and ingredients in one basket. A first aid kit for stains should include the following:

- Baking Soda
- Club Soda
- Cornstarch
- Cotton Balls
- Cream of Tartar
- Dishwashing Soap (Clear)
- Distilled White Vinegar
- Salt, Both Table and Kosher
- Hydrogen Peroxide
- Liquid Laundry Soap
- Petroleum Jelly
- Rubbing Alcohol
- Plastic Spoon
- Eyedropper

GO
NATURAL

All the stain-removing solutions here use only natural ingredients. Commercial laundry products are among the most caustic, endangering our environment and our families. These more responsible methods work on all washable fabrics. And don't give up too quickly—it sometimes takes patience and several tries before a stain comes out.

STAIN	METHOD FOR REMOVAL
BABY FORMULA SPIT-UP	Gently scrape away excess surface spittle with a plastic spoon. Sprinkle with baking soda, then pour club soda over the baking soda. Once the fizzing stops, launder, then air-dry. If the stain is still there, repeat.
BIRD DROPPINGS	Scrape away droppings with a plastic spoon. Hold the stained fabric under cold running water. On colorfast fabrics, apply hydrogen peroxide with an eyedropper and rinse.
BLOOD	Hold the spot under cold running water for a minute to rinse out excess blood. Soak in cold water for 30 minutes. Apply dishwashing liquid to the stain. Gently work the soap into the stain and rinse with cold water. Repeat until the stain is gone.
CANDLE WAX	Scrape off excess wax with a plastic spoon. (If the wax is still soft, put fabric in the freezer to harden the wax.) On an ironing board, sandwich the fabric between paper towels or brown paper bags. Set an iron on low heat with no steam. Apply the iron, whose heat will transfer the wax to the paper towel or the bag. Repeat as necessary with new towels or bags. If a stain remains because of colored wax, apply a small amount of rubbing alcohol to the stain, dab, and rinse with cold water. Repeat until the stain is gone.
CHOCOLATE	Scrape chocolate off with a plastic spoon. Dab to remove any liquid. Carefully rub liquid laundry detergent on the stain so as not to spread it. Let the detergent sit for 5 to 10 minutes. Soak it in cold water for 15 minutes. The stain should be gone, but if not, repeat the process until it is.
COLA	Use a cloth or paper towel to remove as much liquid as possible, then apply white vinegar to the spot and blot. Add a small amount of diluted dishwashing liquid and gently work it in. Rinse well and blot to remove excess moisture. If the stain is still apparent, treat with hydrogen peroxide from an eyedropper and let it stand for an hour, then rinse.
CRAYON	Put the garment in a plastic bag, then place in the freezer for 30 minutes to harden the wax before gently scraping excess off. On an ironing board, sandwich the fabric between paper towels or brown paper bags with the crayon side down. With the iron on a low setting and no steam, place the iron on the top towel or bag. As the crayon melts, it will transfer to the bottom towel or bag, so replace it often. Repeat as necessary with new towels or bags.

STAIN	METHOD FOR REMOVAL
DEODORANT	Rub deodorant streaks off clothes with nylon hose, cotton socks, or soft foam (the kind that comes on metal hangers from dry cleaners).
FECES	Scrape off as much as possible with a plastic spoon. Rinse under cold running water. Fill a basin with water as hot as the fabric can tolerate; add 1 c. hydrogen peroxide and 1 c. baking soda. Agitate as much as possible, so the solution can dislodge the stain. Let it soak overnight. If the stain is gone, launder with laundry detergent. Air-dry.
GRASS	Using an eyedropper or cotton ball, pretreat the stain with rubbing alcohol. Rinse in cold water. Make a paste with a small amount of water and 2 tbsp. laundry detergent. Cover the stain and let it sit for 15 to 20 minutes before laundering. Let it air-dry and check to make sure all pigment is gone. If not, apply the paste described in this chart for removing red clay and launder again.
GUM	Fold clothing to fit within a plastic bag; leave the gum exposed on top so it doesn't stick to the bag. Alternatively, lay the fabric on top of a cookie sheet. Place it in the freezer for 3 to 4 hours. Remove and open the bag, and use a plastic spoon to remove the hardened gum.
INK AND PERMANENT MARKER	Contain the ink by applying a circle of petroleum jelly around it. Lay down the ink-contact side of the fabric on a paper towel to absorb the stain. Use an eyedropper to saturate the stain with rubbing alcohol, and dab with cotton balls. Move the towel to a new, dry spot often. Add more alcohol and continue tamping until all is absorbed into the towels. It can take a while. If any ink remains, spot-treat with dishwashing detergent and let it sit 15 to 20 minutes before laundering. Air-dry.
KETCHUP	Scrape off as much as possible without spreading the stain. Run cold water from the back of the stain toward the front so the ketchup does not absorb further into the fibers. Apply laundry detergent to any remaining stain and work it in with your fingers. Consider soaking in cold, soapy water for 30 minutes. Rinse with cold water. If the stain is still visible, apply white vinegar with an eyedropper and repeat, working in dishwashing detergent. Rinse again. If that hasn't cleared the redness, apply a little hydrogen peroxide with an eyedropper and let it sit for a while before working in more dishwashing detergent.
LIPSTICK	Scrape excess lipstick from the surface with the edge of a plastic spoon. Treat the stain from the backside of the garment and place a towel underneath it to absorb the stain. Drop rubbing alcohol from an eyedropper onto the stain and dab with a dry cloth or paper towel. Repeat until all color is gone.
MUD	Let the mud dry and scrape off any excess with a plastic spoon. Apply a small amount of laundry detergent to the stain and work it in. Leave it for 15 minutes. Wet a toothbrush and scrub to loosen the stain, working from both the inside and outside of the fabric. Rinse with cold water when you feel the stain is sufficiently dislodged. Launder and air-dry.

STAIN	METHOD FOR REMOVAL
MUSTARD	Scrape excess mustard from clothing with a plastic spoon. Working with the garment's back side out, use an eyedropper to saturate the area with white vinegar. When most of the color is gone, work dishwashing liquid into the stain and rinse until all color has disappeared. Repeat with white vinegar and liquid soap if needed.
OIL	Immediately sprinkle cornstarch onto the stain to absorb the oil. Let sit for 15 minutes, then brush away and saturate the spot with rubbing alcohol. Blot away excess moisture and work liquid dishwashing soap into the stain. Rinse well, and repeat with rubbing alcohol if necessary.
PERSPIRATION STAINS	On white or light garments, mix 1 c. hydrogen peroxide with 1 c. water in a spray bottle and saturate the stain. Let it sit for 30 minutes. Rinse and launder in cold water. For darker staining on light garments, consider adding 1 c. hydrogen peroxide to a normal laundry load. For colored fabrics that may get bleached by hydrogen peroxide, mix 2 tbsp. white vinegar with 1 c. water and saturate the stained area. Let it sit for 30 minutes before laundering.
RED CLAY	Scrape dried clay off with a plastic spoon and a dry toothbrush. On colored fabric, make a paste of $1/4$ c. table salt to $1/4$ c. white vinegar. Apply it to the stain and let rest for 20 minutes. Rinse off the paste and launder normally. Repeat if the stain has not disappeared. On white fabric, mix 1 tbsp. cream of tartar, 1 tsp. baking soda, and just enough lemon juice to form a paste. Apply it to the stain and leave the fabric in the sun until the paste dries. Scrape off the paste. Launder normally and air-dry. Repeat if the stain persists.
RED WINE	Club soda won't remove red wine, but it can make it easier to clean later, so it's still a good emergency measure if you're out at a restaurant. At home, pour table salt on the stain and let it rest for an hour. Pour boiling water through the stain. Repeat as needed.
RUST	Lay fabric on an old towel and pour white vinegar or lemon juice on the stain (or make a paste of salt and lemon juice). Blot the stain with a clean white towel, and repeat if necessary. Lay fabric in direct sun, and once the stain disappears, launder and air-dry.
SOY SAUCE	Blot stain with a clean white cloth. Rinse from the back side of the fabric. Dab the front of the stain with white vinegar, then hydrogen peroxide. Let it sit, then rinse. Launder normally and air-dry.
TOOTHPASTE	Carefully scrape away toothpaste from stain with a plastic spoon. Apply detergent and water to a clean cloth or sponge and dab toothpaste until it disappears, then rinse.
URINE	Fill a bucket or the sink with 1 part white vinegar to 2 parts hot water (cold water if the fabric is delicate). Soak the urine-stained fabric for 45 minutes. Remove and rinse. If the stain is gone, launder using laundry detergent and air-dry.
WATER-BASED GLUE	Let the glue dry. Soak in room-temperature water for 24 hours to soften. Wipe glue with a clean, dry cloth to protect fabric that might weaken with scrubbing. Launder normally in warm water and air-dry.

243 KEEP COLD

Most everyday clothes can be washed on cold to minimize sorting and save on energy costs. Also, use a light hand when adding your laundry detergent. When it comes to soap, more doesn't always mean better, and too much detergent can leave residue on your clothes and overload your washing machine with suds. For small- to regular-sized loads, 1 tbsp. of detergent (liquid or powdered) is enough. For an extra-large load, you can bump it up to 2 tbsp. If your clothes are heavily soiled, utilize the presoak and extra rinse settings on your washer instead of adding more soap.

244 WASH THE WASHER

All that warm water mixed with dirty fabrics takes a toll on the machine and can foster mold and mildew—something that often goes unnoticed until your clothes develop a musty smell. For deep cleaning, add 1 c. bleach directly into the drum (per the manufacturer's instructions), and then run the machine on its hottest cycle. Check your owner's manual before doing a similar deep cleaning.

245 DECODE COMMON LAUNDRY SYMBOLS

Universal laundry symbols are increasingly replacing written care instructions on garment tags. In a global economy, a knit shirt manufactured in one country may be shipped to six nations with different languages. Universal pictograms graphically illustrate the cleaning processes best suited to the fabric. Here's a primer on how to read the symbols.

WASH	BLEACH	TUMBLE DRY	DRY	IRON	DRY CLEAN
(basin)	(triangle)	(circle in square)	(square)	(iron)	(circle)
Cool/Cold	Any Bleach	No Heat	Line Dry	Low	Do Not Dry Clean
Warm	Nonchlorine	Low	Drip Dry	Medium	
Hot	No Bleach	Medium	Dry Flat	High	
Normal		High	Dry in Shade	No Steam	
Permanent Press		Any Heat	Do Not Dry	Do Not Iron	
Delicate		Do Not Tumble Dry	Do Not Wring		
Hand-Wash					
Do Not Wash					

246 KNOW WHAT THE NUMBERS MEAN

It's simple to understand the care symbols of a shirt you bought during your Paris vacation or the blouse ordered from a Spanish website. The European wash-temperature symbols indicate the maximum recommended water temperature in Celsius, and sometimes use horizontal bars instead of vertical bars for the recommended type of cycle. It's that easy!

247 SOFTEN UP

You can achieve soft towels and clothes without the challenges that accompany chemical fabric softeners. Liquid fabric softener—as well as dryer sheets—coat your clothes with chemical compounds that cause the threads to extend, creating that luxurious fluffy softness. But that coating can build up and make fibers less absorbent. Instead, simply put $^1/_2$ c. white vinegar in the fabric softener dispenser so it's added during the rinse cycle. The white vinegar is just acidic enough to dissolve fabric softener buildup as well as detergent residue and hard-water mineral deposits that make towels feel scratchy and rough. Adding this small amount of vinegar to your rinse cycle will make your clothes soft, smell fresh, and be fully absorbent.

QUICK TIP

USE YOUR JUDGMENT

The symbols identify the most aggressive cleaning possible without damaging a garment, but you can use gentler methods and temperatures if you think it best. For instance, the symbol may indicate that hot water is acceptable, but you may prefer to wash in warm or cold water. And if you like the whitening power of industrial bleach, but are wary of its harsh chemicals, try using this Bleaching Solution instead—it's much less toxic and can help brighten your whites!

BLEACHING SOLUTION

1 c. hydrogen peroxide

$^1/_4$ c. lemon juice

3 qt. water

Thoroughly mix all ingredients in a large container. Pour 1 to 2 c. per wash load into the bleach dispenser.

248 STRIP YOUR LAUNDRY

When your laundry still seems dirty and stinky, despite being "clean," it's time to strip them. This process removes soap residue, mineral buildup from hard water, and body oils that have accumulated over time in things like workout clothes, towels, sports equipment, and bedding. Here's how you do it:

LAUNDRY STRIPPER

$^1/_4$ c. borax

$^1/_4$ c. washing soda

$^1/_2$ c. powdered laundry detergent

Fill your bathtub with hot water and add all ingredients, stir until they're dissolved, then add the washed and dried clothes or linens. Swish the mixture around every hour for 4 to 6 hours, then drain the bathtub and wash the laundry in a regular cycle in your washing machine (no detergent needed).

Front-load washing machines use less energy and water, but they can smell funky if they are not cleaned often. The rubber gasket around the door of front-loaders is more substantial than on top-loaders because it must hold back sloshing water. It's in that gasket that mold and mildew thrive on moisture and soap residue. Some models have a self-cleaning option, but you should still check the gasket for mold.

STEP ONE Wipe the rubber gasket (and whatever area around the gasket you can reach) with the Nonabrasive Vinegar Cleaner (see tip 239) and a microfiber cloth. Pull the gasket back to clean the inside where mold grows. Because acidic vinegar can potentially deteriorate some rubber, wash the gasket, inside and out, with a wet cloth. Dry with a clean microfiber cloth to halt the growth of mold.

STEP TWO Select settings for a large load, extra-heavy soiling, and hot water. Fill the detergent dispenser to its maximum level with vinegar (or use $3/4$ c., whichever is greater) and start the cycle. Also, run a second cycle on rinse to make sure all the vinegar is removed from the drum.

STEP THREE Remove all dispensers (detergent, bleach, and fabric softener) and filters and wash them in the sink in warm, soapy water. Rinse, dry, and replace.

STEP FOUR Spray the Nonabrasive Vinegar Cleaner (see tip 239) onto a microfiber cloth and wipe the exterior. Scrub tight, dirty areas with a toothbrush.

250 TAKE IT FROM THE TOP

If you have a top-load washer, follow these suggestions for cleaning your machine (after you've checked your owner's manual). A top-loader's design requires a different approach in order to clean the top of the tub.

STEP ONE Set the cycle for the hottest temperature, largest load, and maximum soil level, then start the machine. Once it's full of water, add 1 qt. vinegar. Let the machine do its thing for several minutes to mix the solution. Pause the cycle by opening the lid.

STEP TWO Let the machine rest for 1 to 2 hours to let the vinegar work on the mold and mildew before restarting the machine to finish its cycle. Run an additional rinse to make certain that all the vinegar drains out of the drum.

STEP THREE Remove all dispensers (detergent, bleach, and fabric softener) and filters and wash them in the sink in warm, soapy water. Rinse, dry completely, and replace.

STEP FOUR Spray the Nonabrasive Vinegar Cleaner (see tip 239) onto a microfiber cloth and wipe the exterior. Scrub tight, dirty areas with a toothbrush.

251 SHOW YOUR DRYER SOME LOVE

The hug of warm towels that emerge fresh from the dryer is something to look forward to. And the more quickly you collect the laundry once the dryer cycle ends, the less ironing and smoothing you'll have to do later. But dryers need maintenance or the lint filter can become a fire hazard. And even if you always clean the lint filter, fibers will inevitably get through and clog your exhaust line over time.

252 CUT DRY TIME

Shrink dry time and energy costs by tossing a clean, dry towel in the dryer with a load of wet clothes. It will help absorb moisture and help clothes dry more quickly.

253 ADD A LITTLE BOUNCE

Dryer balls, by bouncing around among your clothes and pushing individual garments apart, create better air circulation. But they can also be used to add a fresh scent in lieu of dryer sheets.

ADD Toss three wool dryer balls and a load of wet clothes into the dryer. Run the dryer cycle as usual.

SCENT Once the load is dry, take the dryer balls out and add 1 to 2 drops of essential oil such as lemongrass or lavender to each wool ball.

TUMBLE Throw the dryer balls back into the dryer with the load and run on the no-heat cycle for 5 minutes, which will enable the delightful scents to transfer to your clothes.

254 KEEP DRYER VENTS CLEAN

The dryer's venting system is designed to exhaust heat and moisture to the outside. Even if you consistently clear the lint trap, lint particles can accumulate at other places along the exhaust system—as fine as your lint screen is, some lint particles will still be finer. One early tip-off to a clogged vent is that your clothes don't seem to dry in one cycle. Rather than risk a fire, attend to the dryer every 6 months.

DISASSEMBLE Unplug the dryer and pull it away from the wall. Remove the exhaust hose. If it's flexible, scrunch it up and vacuum inside, or clean the inside with a rag.

CLEAR Depending on the make of your dryer, you may have to take off the entire back panel, or you may be able to remove only the vent clamp and duct off the back. Reach into the vent on the back and pull out as much lint as you can. With a dust-brush attachment, vacuum any lint or dust you see. Vacuum the floor, then mop it and dry it before reattaching all parts and pushing the dryer back into place.

CLEAN Spray the drum with the Nonabrasive Vinegar Cleaner (see tip 239) and wipe clean with a microfiber cloth. Wash the lint filter in warm, soapy water, scrubbing nasty corners with a toothbrush. While it's out, vacuum the lint that accumulates in its cavity. If possible, remove the lint-trap cover and vacuum.

RETURN Rinse and dry completely before replacing the filter. Spray the exterior and control panels with the Nonabrasive Vinegar Cleaner and wipe it clean with a microfiber cloth.

255 FILTER OUT LINT

What exactly is lint? It's not just stray threads from garments but also tiny fragments of threads and fibers formed from everyday wear, as well as fiber fragments from those stray receipts that somehow get past your laundry vigilance. Unlike fabric, in which long fibers are woven together and overlap, lint's fibers are short and independent, so there is much more surface area exposed. And that transforms all the individual fibers into a collection of kindling, which can ignite from the dryer's heat.

QUICK TIP

JUST USE HALF

If dryer sheets are a habit you just can't (or don't want to) break, you can stretch them twice as long simply by tearing each one in half. A half dryer sheet is still plenty effective for the average load of laundry, and you'll save on money and waste.

256 MAKE YOUR OWN DRYER SHEETS

If you don't use dryer balls but still want to add a natural fragrance to your laundry, add 8 drops of essential oil to a cotton cloth and add it in the dryer clothes after they have dried. Circulate on a no-heat cycle for 5 minutes and you will have a fresh scent!

CHECKLISTS

Chances are good that your daily and weekly laundry routines are pretty well established. If you're not giving your laundry room the attention it needs to stay in tip-top working order, use this list to set up a maintenance schedule. Numbers refer to the general cleaning tips, so make sure to reference the appropriate supporting tips to address specific materials and circumstances.

DAILY
☐ Sweep or vacuum floors 039
☐ Declutter laundry room 227
☐ Spot-treat stains 242
☐ Wash clothes 227
☐ Dry clothes 253

WEEKLY
☐ Dust window treatments 019
☐ Dust doors and baseboards 023
☐ Clean switch plates 024
☐ Dust ceilings and walls 026
☐ Mop floors 040
☐ Wipe down washer and dryer
☐ Clean lint filter 254, 255

MONTHLY
☐ Clean window treatments 019
☐ Wash trash cans 037
☐ Clean doorknobs 038
☐ Clean washer 246, 249, 250
☐ Clean sink 197
☐ Sweep and mop behind washer and dryer
☐ Wipe down washer and dryer 254

SEASONALLY (SPRING AND FALL)
☐ Wash windows 017
☐ Deep clean window treatments 019
☐ Wipe doors and baseboards 023
☐ Clean walls 026
☐ Clean sconces and light fixtures 067, 070
☐ Clean iron 237
☐ Clean washer 246, 249, 250
☐ Clean dryer vent 254
☐ Restock laundry supplies 239, 241
☐ Clean lint filter 255

257 LOVE YOUR LIVING ROOM

Whether your living room is formal or a more casual, this is the spot where you gather for conversation, cocktail parties, breakfast meetings, and socializing. It should be as pretty as it is comfortable, and it's one of those rooms that should always be ready for company. You never know who will show up! Take a pass over furniture and décor every few days to keep dust and cobwebs at bay. Keep it simple and use a slightly dampened microfiber cloth, working from top to bottom.

258 INCLUDE THE KIDS

Handheld cleaning tools are a wonderful way to involve little ones in the work of housekeeping. Keep lint rollers, a microfiber dusting mitt, a handheld broom and dustpan, and a hand vacuum handy so they can assist in cleaning up crumbs and small messes.

259 KEEP WORK SPACES CLEAR

Many remote workers without dedicated home offices work from their living rooms. Whether you're set up at a desk or with a tray table on the sofa, at the end of your workday, try to clean off the surface. Otherwise, it's easy to feel like you're never escaping the responsibilities of your job.

260 SAVE NEWSPAPER

A classic recyclable, last week's Sunday paper can also help you save money in the long run if you use it to replace wrapping paper. Of course, you'll want to pull out any depressing articles, but what's left can be interesting, playful, and a fun element if you're able to somehow match the topic to the recipient's interests. Pair it with a colorful ribbon for a present that pops.

261 CLEAR HORIZONTAL SURFACES

To avoid visual clutter, consider keeping at least some horizontal surfaces completely clear. Not every tabletop needs to have a decoration on top of it. Flat, empty spaces send a message of being available for all the stuff of life—work, play, and meals—without needing to be freed up first or reset when you're done.

262 REPURPOSE CANDLE JARS

Instead of tossing old candle containers, clean them out and reuse them as storage, vases, or gifts. First, scoop out as much leftover wax as possible with a spoon or butter knife. Then, gently heat the container in a double boiler to melt any remaining wax. Pour out the remaining wax, and then while the container is still warm, carefully wipe it out with a paper towel. Repeat the process as necessary, then wash the container by hand in your sink using dish soap and hot water.

263 HAVE A BLANKET BASKET

A basket for throw blankets makes pickup easy for kids—and grownups!

264 MOVE FURNITURE WITH EASE

Pulling your furniture away from the walls is essential for a thorough cleaning, and you never know what you might find back there. However, if your sofas and tables are heavy, furniture sliders come in handy. Tilt or lift the piece to position these small pads beneath it. They will cut down on the friction and allow your furniture to glide across the floor.

265 DEEP CLEAN YOUR SOFA

Between everyday use that wears and fades upholstered furniture and spills that leave a mark, the sofa gets a lot of wear. You can always send it out to be dry-cleaned, but a more efficient and environmentally responsible alternative is cleaning the sofa yourself.

STEP ONE Find the manufacturer's care tag on the sofa to see its recommended method of overall cleaning. (See tip 266 for help in decoding the care instructions.)

STEP TWO Vacuum the sofa surface, the cushions, the sofa body below the cushions (where pocket change and remote controls hide), and behind and under the sofa. Then brush with a bristled brush, dislodging any dirt, following the path of the vacuum so as not to miss any area. Vacuum the dislodged dirt.

STEP THREE Go over the sofa and cushions with a lint roller, following the path of the vacuum and brush. This will pull up stubborn pet hair and fur and resistant dust.

STEP FOUR Spray the All-Purpose Cleaner (see tip 267) on a microfiber cloth to clean exposed wood and metal areas.

STEP FIVE Once you have vacuumed every trace of dust, surface dirt, and hair from the furniture, attack the stains by spot-cleaning. If the manufacturer's code is a "W" or "SW" (see tip 266), you can escalate treatment with a steam cleaner per its instructions.

266 KNOW THE CODE

Much like how laundry garments have symbols to communicate washing and drying instructions, upholstery has its own cleaning language. Use the key below to understand what the care letters mean:

O Clean with cold water, because it's made from organic materials.

S Clean only with a solvent-based cleanser—such as denatured alcohol—or dry-clean. Do not use water or water-based products.

SW Clean with a solvent-based cleaner and/or water-based cleanser.

V Wash regularly with warm water and mild soap. Do not use harsh cleaning products.

W Clean with water or a water-based solvent or foam.

X Clean only with a vacuum, or hire a professional.

If the sofa has been reupholstered or you have lost its care instructions, test an inconspicuous area to see how water affects the fabric. Then clean according to the tips below.

CLEAN AND POLISH
THE WHOLE HOME

Keep a batch of these natural cleaning products on hand to deal with accidents and maintain clean surfaces.

NOTE: Remember that while natural cleaners can be useful for cleaning and getting that sparkle and shine, they don't quite cut it for sanitizing germy surfaces. For that, turn to an all-purpose cleaner. There are several plant-based disinfectants that are effective at killing bacteria and viruses.

ALL-PURPOSE CLEANER

2 tsp. borax

$1/4$ tsp. liquid castile soap

10 drops lemon essential oil

Mix all ingredients with hot water in a 16-oz. spray bottle.

GLASS CLEANER

$1/4$ c. distilled white vinegar

5 drops lemon essential oil

Mix all ingredients with hot water in a 16-oz. spray bottle.

FURNITURE POLISH

$1/2$ c. jojoba oil

2 tbsp. distilled white vinegar

5 drops lemon essential oil

Pour the all ingredients in a sealable 8-oz. jar. Vigorously shake to emulsify before using.

NONABRASIVE VINEGAR CLEANER

1 part distilled white vinegar

2 parts water

5 drops essential oil

Combine the vinegar and water in a 16-oz. spray bottle. Add 5 drops of essential oil such as lavender, grapefruit, orange, lemon, or peppermint if you don't like the smell of vinegar.

268 ATTACK THE STAIN

The cleaning codes should be considered to determine whether to use a solvent-based or water-based cleaner when spot-treating a stain, and adapting them with the laundry stain guide (see tip 242) can yield a custom solution. Minimize the amount of liquid so it doesn't supersaturate the furniture, and always test on a small, inconspicuous area.

269 FRESHEN UP

Baking soda is the go-to method for freshening upholstery. Using a cheese shaker, sprinkle a thin layer of baking soda over cushions and upholstered surfaces. Let it sit for at least 15 minutes or overnight, vacuum clean, and the stale smell will disappear.

270 SHAMPOO UPHOLSTERY

Unless your upholstery is coded "S" or "X" and is not water tolerant, a simple shampoo can help lift out unsightly marks.

SUDS Create a foam by whipping together equal parts dishwashing liquid and water. Apply the foam to the stain.

RUB Gently work the foam into the stain with your fingertips so as not to strain the fabric. Let it sit for 5 minutes.

REMOVE Rinse a sponge with water and apply water to the stain to remove the soapy foam. Blot dry with a microfiber cloth. You may have to repeat on stubborn stains.

DRY Soak up as much moisture as you can with a microfiber cloth. Let air-dry completely.

271 REFRESH MICROFIBER

Microfiber is a popular upholstery fabric due to its durability, but it's notorious for showing water spots and stains. The best way to clean it is by spraying it with rubbing alcohol. Working quickly, use a brush or the rough side of a sponge to scrub it clean. Let it dry thoroughly before fluffing it with a brush in a circular motion.

272 OPT FOR A SLIPCOVER

For the easiest way to protect your sofa or refresh a piece of furniture that's seen better days, a slipcover is hard to beat. Relaxed or fitted, they're available in a variety of styles to fit your design taste. Most can be machine-washed in cold water, and then air-dried, coming out looking good as new!

273 CARE FOR FINE LEATHER

Leather ages over time and with use. It takes on an attractive patina, but still needs regular cleaning to keep it in top shape. When you turn your attention to leather furniture, be mindful of where it sits in your room: Keep it out of direct sunlight and away from vents, both of which will dry and weaken the leather.

STEP ONE Clean as you did according to the entry for nonleather upholstery (see tip 265), vacuuming dust and dirt and running a lint roller over any remaining pet hair.

STEP TWO Wipe it down with a dry microfiber cloth. Fill a bucket with equal parts white vinegar and water. Wet a microfiber cloth so it's damp but not saturated. Wipe the leather sofa cushions and body, repeatedly rinsing the cloth and dipping it in the cleaning solution.

STEP THREE Dry the leather with a clean cloth—water that sits on the leather will stain and weaken the upholstery.

274 TREAT STAINS ON LEATHER

Leather furniture is expensive, so it can be scary when you notice marks on the upholstery. Follow these guidelines to help put yourself at ease.

GREASE Sprinkle baking soda on the stained area. Let it sit for a few hours, then brush it off with a clean rag.

INK Dip a cotton swab in rubbing alcohol and dab the swab on the ink stain. Make sure to lightly apply the alcohol to minimize the ink spreading.

DARK SPOTS ON LIGHT LEATHER Make a paste of equal parts cream of tartar and lemon juice. Apply paste to the spot and leave on for 10 minutes, then wipe the leather with a damp cloth and let air-dry.

275 REPAIR LEATHER SCRATCHES

Scratches that you can barely see can be buffed away with a soft cloth and leather conditioner. Apply a leather conditioner, wait 10 minutes for it to soak in, then gently rub in a circular motion. For deeper scratches, contact the manufacturer to see if they can give you a color-matching balm or restoration kit.

276 REMEMBER THROW PILLOWS AND BLANKETS

Because they're not on your bed, these pillows and blankets are easier to overlook when it comes to cleaning. At least seasonally, give them a good once-over. If you have kids or pets in the home, you may find you need to do this more often. If the pillow cover can be removed from the insert, take it off before washing. As always, check care tags for the best washing instructions. Replace any deflated pillow inserts with new ones.

277 OPT FOR A NATURAL POLISH

Commercial furniture polishes contain chemicals that aren't good choices for use in our homes. They're not good for recently manufactured furniture, either; they will dim—and can damage—the factory finish. Use the Furniture Polish (see tip 267) to create a lustrous shine that doesn't feel oily. Once a month, dip a corner of a microfiber cloth in the polish and rub it on with a brisk circular motion, then buff with a dry microfiber cloth.

278 DUST WOOD OFTEN

Wooden pieces manufactured in the past 50 years have a hard, clean finish that protects the surface and maintains sheen. Resist applying commercial polishes that can damage the factory finish. The best care you can give your wood furniture is to actually do as little as possible. Wipe their surfaces weekly with a barely damp microfiber cloth to pick up dust, and leave it at that.

279
TRY
A PEN

Touch up scratches in your wood with wood repair markers. They come in a range of colors, so it's quite easy to get a very close match. They're inexpensive, convenient, and can really rejuvenate a piece of beat-up wooden furniture.

280
GO BEYOND
DUSTING

Wooden coffee tables and end tables may accumulate more than dust over time and need an occasional cleaning. Put 1 tbsp. castile soap into 1 qt. water, wet a microfiber cloth or soft sponge, and squeeze most of the moisture out before washing the surface. Follow with a second clean, damp cloth to remove any soap residue. Dry to avoid water spots and streaks.

281
TEND TO
YOUR FIREPLACE

Deep clean the fireplace at least twice per year, and clean out the ashes weekly while in use. It's also important to have it inspected and professionally cleaned once a year—for recommendations, check the website for the Chimney Safety Institute of America.

 CLEAN THE FIREBOX

It takes three days for embers to completely cool, so if embers remain, wait at least that long after you have a fire to start cleaning. Avoid extinguishing a fire by dowsing with water, because it will produce a lot of smoke and make ash hard.

CLEAR Remove everything from the fireplace: the fireplace screen and cover, tools, grate, andirons or chenets, and unburnt logs if you have them. Open the flue.

SPREAD Put wet coffee grounds on top of the fireplace ashes to prevent the ashes from flying into the air when you clean them out of the fireplace.

REMOVE Shovel and sweep the ashes together and put them in a sturdy bag or tin, preferably with a lid so they don't spread dust into the air. Sweep everywhere—top, bottom, back, and sides. Move ashes onto your compost pile outside.

VACUUM Use the dust-brush attachment to vacuum the interior top, bottom, back, sides, and the damper ledge, as well as the exterior of the fireplace and surround. Periodically clean the dust-brush attachment so that you don't transfer soot from one area to another. Clean the dust brush again when finished.

LOOSEN If the firebox is relatively new and doesn't have a thick coating of soot, spraying with the All-Purpose Cleaner (see tip 267) will loosen it. Scrub the interior with a stiff brush, rinsing the brush in water when needed, then use a rag to wipe up the grime.

CUSTOMIZE Identify the material of your firebox, and follow the appropriate directions in tip 284.

283 GET THE TOOLS

Cleaning the fireplace is a dirty job, and you'll need the right supplies to do a thorough job. Grab a drop cloth, gloves, a breathing mask, goggles, a scrub brush, rags, the vacuum, and microfiber cloths.

284 DEEP CLEAN FIREBOXES

Whether you have a built-in masonry fireplace or a factory-built fireplace, regular seasonal cleaning will keep them beautiful and ready for the next chilly evening.

BRICK The firebox in traditional, built-in masonry fireplaces is lined with firebrick, which can withstand high temperatures. Cleaning it is a messy job, but one you can do yourself. Cover the surrounding floor and furniture with drop cloths, and use a dust mask and work gloves. Mix 1 part salt to 1 part mild dish-washing liquid or castile soap. Add just enough water to make a thick paste, and apply the paste to the wall with your hands. Let the paste sit for 10 to 15 minutes and scrub with a stiff-bristled brush. Remove residue with a wet sponge, rinsing it often, and repeat the process as necessary.

METAL AND CERAMIC Factory-built fireplaces use metal and ceramic liners in the firebox that are less likely to accumulate soot and easier to clean. Your vacuum's dust-brush attachment will usually remove any soot or dirt. Follow with soap and water if needed.

You should also hire a professional chimney sweep to clear the creosote from the chimney after each fire-burning season.

285 CLEAN A GAS FIREPLACE

Although gas fireplaces do not leave the ash of their wood-burning cousins, they still create a bit of soot from particles in the air. Follow these directions to maintain a tidy appearance.

STEP ONE Turn off the gas valve and wait for the firebox to cool.

STEP TWO Vacuum the firebox area, looking for dust, dirt, cobwebs, and anything else in the area. Check the valves, burners, and control area to be sure nothing could prevent its safe operation.

STEP THREE Vacuum in and around ceramic logs or any other items used to disperse the heat. If there are any small pieces like lava rocks, cover the attachment with cheesecloth or hosiery to prevent small pieces from getting sucked into the vacuum.

STEP FOUR Spray a clean microfiber cloth with the Glass Cleaner (see tip 267) and wipe the interior of the screen. Use a new cloth and fresh spray to clean the exterior.

286 REMEMBER THE ACCESSORIES

If it's too cold to clean the fireplace accessories outside, consider doing so in the bathtub. Just remember to lay a towel in the tub to protect the surface and another one on the floor to protect it.

LOOSEN Spray a microfiber cloth with the All-Purpose Cleaner (see tip 267) and wipe the tools to eliminate the surface dirt and soot.

SOAK Lay a towel in the bathtub, move the fireplace accessories into the tub, and fill it with warm, soapy water.

CLEAN Scrub the accessories—mesh fireplace screen, andirons, chenets, grate—with a scrub brush, toothbrush, or microfiber cloth. Rinse and thoroughly dry.

287 MIND THE MANTEL

Smoke and soot will inevitably darken your fireplace surround and mantel. It's a fairly easy process to clean, but knowing whether your material is sealed is important. To get started, take everything off the mantel and take down any art hanging overhead. Keep the cleaning materials from tip 283 handy, and follow the appropriate directions below for your surround material.

STONE Dip a microfiber cloth or sponge in warm, soapy water and scrub. Rinse with a water-dampened cloth and thoroughly dry.

BRICK Follow the directions for cleaning brick in tip 284.

WOOD Wipe with a warm, soapy solution on a microfiber cloth. Rinse with a clean, damp microfiber cloth. Make sure to thoroughly dry afterward, as standing water on wood will leave a mark.

METAL Spray the surface with the Nonabrasive Vinegar Cleaner (see tip 267) and wipe with a microfiber cloth, always moving in the direction of the grain. Apply baby oil and wipe it off. Resistant stains can be cleaned with a baking soda paste; apply and then rub off in the direction of the grain.

CONCRETE Dip a microfiber cloth or sponge in warm, soapy water and scrub. Rinse with a clean, damp cloth, then thoroughly dry. If the concrete is sealed, use a soft-bristled scrub brush.

TILE Dip a microfiber cloth or sponge in warm, soapy water and scrub. Rinse with a clean, damp cloth and thoroughly dry. Clean grout with a grout brush and a paste of baking soda and hydrogen peroxide (see tip 185).

288 WIPE FIREPLACE GLASS CLEAN

Vacuum the firebox-facing glass to remove any ashes or dirt. Spray a microfiber cloth with the Glass Cleaner (see tip 267) and wipe the glass. This will require a little elbow grease and repeat sprays in order to break down the soot. Use a razor blade if you can't get a piece of dirt to come loose, and swap in a new cloth when one gets dirty. Do the same process on the front-facing side, which should be much easier!

289 PRESERVE OLD FURNITURE

Inherited or acquired, your antique wooden furniture requires a hands-off approach. If you've ever seen *Antiques Roadshow*, you know that a bad cleaning or restoration can do permanent damage and reduce the value and marketability of your prized antique. Older furniture with an oiled finish does best with regular dusting only; never apply polish or wax. If the wood becomes dry, it needs to be re-oiled. If your antique already has a wax finish, it must be waxed again and energetically buffed every 6 months to keep its shine. Don't use soap or oil polishes on top of wax. With all antiques, take a little more care when dusting to prevent accidental damage. Many museums have days devoted to assessing people's antiques and providing advice. If you're unsure how to maintain an ornate or valuable piece of furniture, check whether a museum has a conservation department or if a curator can refer you to a nearby expert in restoration and preservation.

290 TAKE CARE OF YOUR TV

Whether you have weekly family movie night or binge-watch the latest hit, your TV sees a lot of action. Give it the care it deserves, and dust it weekly to keep the picture sharp and the operation efficient. Before you get started, unplug the electronics and wait until the TV cools down.

CATHODE-RAY TUBE TV The old type of TV with the clunky back still gets some use. To clean, spray a microfiber cloth with the Glass Cleaner (see tip 267) and wipe the front and back clean. Dry with a clean microfiber cloth.

PLASMA, LCD, LED, REAR-PROJECTION SCREEN These screens are super sensitive, so dust them with a clean, dry microfiber cloth. Wipe down the front, back, and buttons to prevent any dust from collecting. If the dust is resistant, dampen a clean microfiber cloth with distilled water and wipe the surface lightly in wide circles. If there are fingerprints or any stubborn goo, use a solution of 1 part distilled white vinegar to 1 part distilled water. Spray a microfiber cloth and wipe the spotted area, then let it air-dry.

291 DEEP CLEAN YOUR SPEAKERS

Speakers are designed to disappear into your living room, so it's natural to overlook them. Use the upholstery-brush attachment on a low setting to vacuum the fabric cover, and vacuum the back of the cover if its removable. Use a lint roller to collect any resistant dust. For any nonfabric areas of the speaker cabinet, dampen a clean microfiber cloth with water and wipe away any dust, then let the speakers air-dry.

292 TAKE CONTROL OF THE REMOTE

We've already emphasized cleaning the remote when you have a sick family member (see tip 226), but it's a good tool to keep clean regardless!

STEP ONE Remove the batteries to avoid a shock or damaging the electronics.

STEP TWO Use a microfiber cloth dampened with a solution of 1 part alcohol to 1 part distilled water (or use a disposable wipe) to wipe the front, sides, and back of the remote.

STEP THREE Use a cotton swab dipped in the alcohol solution to reach between and on the sides of buttons.

STEP FOUR Let completely air-dry before replacing the batteries.

293 REVIEW YOUR BOOKS

Books are wonderful objects in the home and serve as conversation pieces and reference resources. But they also tend to sit untouched for years at a time. Give them some attention to eliminate common problems, and embrace the idea of editing your collection.

DUST Get rid of the dust on the exteriors of books by wiping with a microfiber cloth. The interior may require opening and a gentle shake to dislodge dust.

BUGS Little insects can make a meal of a book's paper and glue. If bugs have gotten to a book, tightly wrap it in plastic wrap and leave it in the freezer for a few hours to kill the bugs.

MILDEW If you notice mildew spores on the pages, sprinkle cornstarch inside the book and leave it for 1 day before removing.

SCENTS If the book smells musty, stand it up with its pages spread in a covered container with a fresh box of baking soda, and leave for a week.

294 CLEAN THE BOOKSHELVES

To clean bookshelves, first remove the books to have a clear working space. Vacuum the bookshelves using the crevice attachment to get into the corners and wipe clean with a damp microfiber cloth. For resistant dust, spray with the All-Purpose Cleaner (see tip 267). Rinse with a damp cloth and air-dry.

295 LOOK FOR A LITTLE FREE LIBRARY

A little free library in your community is an awesome and convenient way to cull your book collection. You won't have to keep an eye out for special donation days, and your neighbors will appreciate the fresh stock!

296 WASH PET BEDDING

If you have cushions or blankets your pet likes to lay on, be sure to wash them frequently to keep your home smelling fresh. Having a dedicated spot for your dog or cat also keeps their fur and oils off your furniture. When purchasing a bed for your pet, look for one that has a zippered, machine-washable cover.

297 SAVE NATURAL COLLECTIONS

If you love to gather seashells and rocks from your adventures, by all means bring them home. A quick cleaning will keep them special and pre-pared to display. Soak them in water with a squirt of dish soap for 2 hours. Then rinse them well with cold water, and let them soak again in fresh water for 2 more hours. Spread them out on a towel to dry. Leave them natural, or rub them with a tiny bit of mineral oil for shine.

298 CLEAN OUT CLUTTER

If you're trying to develop a more minimalist lifestyle, take a half hour to declutter. Here are some categories you can probably let go of: VHS tapes, CDs, board games you never play, décor you don't like, and textbooks from college.

QUICK TIP

CURATE CAREFULLY

Make your family book sweep an annual event. Donate books that your children have outgrown (libraries love them for annual fundraising sales) or trade them at used bookstores for store credit. Embrace the idea of curating your collection; being more selective about the books you keep elevates their significance!

CHECKLISTS

To convey a welcoming atmosphere to both family and guests, keep clutter out and dust and dirt on the run. Depending on how much use it gets, the living room merits a daily pass-through to guarantee that the space feels fresh. Pick up messes immediately and give it a thorough cleaning every week, so old magazines and tennis shoes under the ottoman don't become permanent. Numbers refer to the general cleaning tips, so make sure to reference the appropriate supporting tips to address specific materials and circumstances.

DAILY
- ☐ Spot-clean spills and potential stains 002, 014, 268, 274
- ☐ Straighten throw pillows 276
- ☐ Sweep or vacuum floors 039

WEEKLY
- ☐ Dust window treatments 019
- ☐ Dust doors and baseboards 023
- ☐ Clean switch plates 024
- ☐ Dust ceilings and walls 026
- ☐ Vacuum carpets and area rugs 052, 054
- ☐ Wipe wooden furniture 278
- ☐ Tend the Fireplace 281, 282, 283, 285, 286, 287, 288
- ☐ Clean remote controls 292
- ☐ Straighten throw pillows 276
- ☐ Dust TV 290

MONTHLY
- ☐ Clean mirrors 018
- ☐ Clean window treatments 019
- ☐ Wash trash cans 037
- ☐ Clean doorknobs 038
- ☐ Vacuum upholstered furniture 265
- ☐ Clean leather upholstery 273
- ☐ Polish wooden furniture 277
- ☐ Dust and clean speakers 291
- ☐ Dust books and bookshelves 293, 294

SEASONALLY (SPRING AND FALL)
- ☐ Wash windows 017
- ☐ Deep clean window treatments 019
- ☐ Wipe doors and baseboards 023
- ☐ Clean walls 026
- ☐ Clean exterior doors 035
- ☐ Deep clean lampshades 066
- ☐ Clean lamp bases 068
- ☐ Clean light fixtures, chandeliers, and sconces 067, 069, 070
- ☐ Deep clean upholstery 265, 270
- ☐ Deep clean fireplace 281, 282, 283, 284, 285, 286, 287, 288
- ☐ Dust lampshades and chandeliers 065, 069
- ☐ Clean and vacuum bookshelves 293, 294
- ☐ Hire a chimney sweep 281, 284, 285

299 EMBRACE THE DINING ROOM

For years, we've heard, "The dining room is dead." It seems everyone wanted more relaxed, casual spaces for entertaining, so walls came down and the grand eat-in kitchen took over. But now people recognize the value of a devoted space for meals. It doesn't have to be formal or fussy, just special so that we can sit, dine, and converse. Still, some dining areas don't see traffic every day, so dust builds up. Mail collects. Piles accumulate. Panic ensues when you plan a party for a room that hasn't seen a cleaning in weeks. Do a quick weekly dusting and a more thorough monthly cleaning, and you'll always be ready for company.

300 THINK BEYOND DINING

In an apartment or small space, your dining table may double as your studio or workspace. If that's the case, store supplies and your printer or scanner in a buffet or nearby cabinet.

301 DECLUTTER YOUR DINING ROOM

Because for many, it's not a frequently used space, the dining room has become a convenient place to hold things that don't belong there. It feels temporary in the moment, but when it's out of sight, it's out of mind, and the next thing you know, it's June and you're that person with a small pile of holiday decorations that didn't get put away. Once a month, go through it and clear out your kids' unfinished art projects, the items you've been meaning to sell, and the abandoned jigsaw puzzle.

302 STORE SMART

Make cleaning your dining room easier by having convenient places to keep serveware and linens. A dining room buffet or china cabinet may seem old fashioned, but they're classic for a reason. Even if you're more casual in nature, it's useful to have your dishes, vases, and candles close at hand.

303 PREPARE FOR GUESTS

Plan a concentrated cleaning twice a year. Anticipate fall and winter holiday dinners, as well as spring religious holidays, when you'll entertain extended family.

RUGS Vacuum the rug as well as the floor. If possible, take both rug and pad outside to air out. Shake out the dust, or if the rug is too large to shake, lay it pile side down and beat the back with a broom to dislodge dust and dirt. If your rug is simply too cumbersome to carry outside, move the dining room table to the side of the room, roll up the rug and pad, and clean the floor underneath.

FLOORS Take advantage of the floor being exposed to give it an extensive cleaning. See tips 043–051 to be confident of the best method for your particular flooring.

WINDOW TREATMENTS Air out draperies, fabric shades, and blinds. Wash or dry-clean if necessary (see tips 019–022).

WINDOWS Wash interior and exterior glass (see tip 017).

CEILINGS AND WALLS Dust is redistributed throughout the house whenever the HVAC unit is heating or cooling and leaves deposits on your ceiling and walls. See tips 026–034 for the most efficient way to restore the true color and finish.

VENTS Wash floor vents in warm, soapy water to minimize dust buildup, and air-dry (see tip 184).

LIGHT FIXTURES Take down ceiling fixtures and sconces for the easiest cleaning. Wash fabric and glass shades following the guidelines in tips 064–068.

304 WASH TABLE LINENS RIGHT

Don't eschew cloth napkins for fear of complex washing—most new cloths can generally go in the washing machine. If there are any stains, identify the food or drink culprits and follow the instructions from tip 242 to spot-treat them. After treating the specific stains, simply load the washing machine with similarly colored linens without overfilling. Wash on the gentle cycle with warm water and select a cold after-rinse.

QUICK TIP

SOFTEN CLOTHS NATURALLY

Commercial fabric softeners weaken fibers and, because table linens need frequent washing, shouldn't be used on them. For a natural fabric softener, put $1/2$ c. white vinegar in the washing machine's fabric softener dispenser so it's added during the rinse cycle.

QUICK TIP

PRESERVE AND PROTECT

Tissue paper, newsprint, cardboard, wood, and even dry-cleaning bags can damage linen and cotton. Vintage linens that have yellowed with thin spots illustrate the results of improper storage. Invest in buffered, acid-free tissue to preserve fine linens. Whether you are hanging, rolling, or folding your linens, put a layer of acid-free tissue beneath the linen; incorporate it with the cloth or napkin as you fold or roll. If you're storing linens on wooden shelves, line the shelves with a double layer of acid-free tissue.

305 HAND-WASH HEIRLOOMS

Older linen cloths, heirlooms, and antiques benefit from hand-washing. If you're just too tired, you can leave them to soak overnight in clean water.

STEP ONE Line the sink (or a large container) with a towel to facilitate lifting the wet linens from the sink later. Fill with ice water and submerge linen napkins and tablecloths.

STEP TWO Grab the four corners of the towel lining the sink and lift the towel, pulling all the linens out of the water along with it. Drain the ice water, and lower the towel-wrapped linens back into the sink.

STEP THREE Spot-treat any stains according to the stain guidelines (see tip 242). Refill the sink with warm water and laundry detergent and return the linens to the sink.

STEP FOUR Carefully agitate the linens in the water (avoiding the temptation to rub or wring linens), then let the linens sit in the soapy water for 15 to 30 minutes. Don't leave linens overnight in soapy water!

STEP FIVE Lift the linens out of the water again using the towel, and drain the sink. Rinse the soap out until water runs clear.

STEP SIX Gently squeeze out excess water and roll the linens in dry towels, squeezing to release more water. Whenever it's practical, line-dry linens. If they're white, put them in the sun; dry colors in the shade. Take them down and iron them while they're still damp.

306 IRON WHILE DAMP

Previous generations sprayed clean clothes with water and then rolled them up until it was time to iron. They did this because it's easier to remove wrinkles in cotton and linen when they are slightly damp. Now you can just take them out of the dryer a little early and skip the extra step.

TREAT DINING ROOM STAINS

When entertaining guests, the best advice for handling a stain is to act quickly to improve your chances of removing it without panicking and causing embarrassment. If someone spills a glass of red wine, just blot away as much as possible, generously sprinkle with table salt, cover with a napkin, and attend to it as soon as guests have left.

DRINK RINGS	
FINISHED WOOD	Apply petroleum jelly or mayonnaise to the ring, and let it sit for 8 to 10 hours before wiping with a microfiber cloth.
UNSEALED WOOD	Buff the stain out of the wood with light sandpaper.
MARBLE	Make a paste of baking soda and water, apply the paste, and cover with plastic wrap for 24 hours. Rinse, dry, and buff.
LINENS (TEA OR COFFEE)	Blot any excess moisture, then apply lemon juice or white vinegar and leave for 5 to 10 minutes. Work dishwashing liquid into the stain, and rinse.
LINENS (RED WINE)	Generously apply table salt and leave for 1 hour, remove the salt, then pour boiling water through the stain. Repeat as needed.
WINE	
FINISHED WOOD	Blot immediately. Apply a paste of equal parts baking soda and either lemon oil or linseed oil. Leave for 30 minutes, wipe off with a damp microfiber cloth, and dry with a clean cloth.
MARBLE	Blot immediately. Apply a paste of equal parts baking soda and water, then cover with plastic wrap for 24 hours. Rinse, dry, and buff.
LINENS	Generously apply table salt and leave for 1 hour, remove the salt, then pour boiling water through the stain. Repeat as needed.
CANDLE WAX	
FINISHED WOOD	Apply a freezer pack or ice cubes in a plastic bag to harden the wax, then gently scrape away with an expired credit card at a 45-degree angle. Treat with the Furniture Polish (see tip 267) and buff with a microfiber cloth.
UNSEALED WOOD	Apply a freezer pack or ice cubes in a plastic bag to harden the wax, then gently scrape away with an expired credit card at a 45-degree angle. If wax has seeped in, cover the spot with layers of paper towels and hold an iron on its lowest setting—with no steam—over the towels to melt the wax and transfer it to the towels.
MARBLE	Apply a freezer pack or ice cubes in a plastic bag to harden the wax, then gently scrape away with an expired credit card at a 45-degree angle. Use warm, soapy water to remove wax residue, then rinse and buff.
GLASS	Gently scrape away with an expired credit card at a 45-degree angle. Warm remaining wax with a hairdryer and scrape. Clean with the Glass Cleaner (see tip 267).
LINENS	Put linens in a large plastic bag, then into the freezer, to harden the wax. Follow instructions for removing wax from unsealed wood. Flush the spot with rubbing alcohol if there's any tint from colored wax.

308 LIFT HEAT TRANSFER STAINS

Have you ever placed something blazing hot on your wooden table and then ended up with a whitish mark? Yikes! Don't worry. This is fixable. Put a damp tea towel over the stain, quickly go over it with an iron on medium-high heat, and then let it cool. It may take a couple passes, but if you're patient, you'll get it out.

309 ENTERTAIN IN AN ECO-FRIENDLY WAY

While traditional, washable flatware, dinnerware, and cloth napkins are undoubtedly the most eco-conscious options, there are some occasions when disposable versions are necessary or make the most sense. Lessen the environmental impact by choosing recycled paper napkins, wooden cutlery, bamboo or compostable plates, and paper straws.

310 CARE FOR FINE CHINA

Whether you have a newly crafted set or your grandmother's gold-edged heirlooms from Europe, delicate porcelain dinnerware brings a sense of elegance to any meal. Preserve this elegance and resist the urge to put china in the dishwasher and risk any chips or fading of intricate designs.

REMOVE Scrape food with a rubber spatula—avoiding metal utensils that may cause damage—then rinse.

PROTECT Line your sink with a towel or a rubber mat to prevent accidental chipping or breaking if a plate drops.

WASH Fill the sink with warm water and a few squirts of mild dishwashing liquid, then use a soft cloth or sponge to clean each piece. Rinse, then dry with a clean microfiber cloth.

311 STORE IT SAFELY

Put a paper towel, coffee filter, felt, or flannel cloth between each plate and store in stacks of no more than five. Such liners will prevent cracking and chipping and stress on plates. Never stack china cups; instead, hang them from specially installed hooks or stand them base down on a shelf to protect the rim.

312 CARE FOR CRYSTAL AND GLASS

When washing fragile crystal and glass, line your sink with a towel or a rubber mat to help prevent chipping or breaking. Add 1 tbsp. distilled white vinegar to your rinse water to prevent water spots on the glass. Store glasses rim up if you use them frequently and rim down if you seldom entertain.

313 ENJOY YOUR SILVER

It's tempting to save your cherished silver for special events only. But using and cleaning your silver every day is the best way to prevent tarnish.

DISHWASHER You can usually wash your sterling silver in the dishwasher as long as you separate it from the stainless flatware—stainless steel will chemically react with silver and permanently stain it. But make sure to remove silver before the dry cycle and instead dry it with a clean, dry towel.

HAND-WASH If you prefer to wash silver flatware by hand, try using a microfiber cloth and mild dishwashing liquid. Silver is soft and can be easily scratched. Don't dump it into a pile in the sink! Thoroughly dry and buff with a clean, dry towel.

SPECIALTY Silver flatware with horn, ebony, or mother-of-pearl handles should not go in the dishwasher. Hand-wash, dry, and shine the handles with olive oil.

314 SHINE SILVERWARE

Regularly polish silver to prevent tarnish and corrosion. If it's correctly stored—in flannel cloths or felt—you buy yourself more time between cleanings. There are plenty of silver polishes on the market, but they give off toxic fumes and require ventilation when polishing. This solution is fast and easy.

STEP ONE Line the kitchen sink or a large roasting pan with aluminum foil, shiny side up, and carefully lay silver pieces on top of the foil to avoid scratching the soft metal. If you use an aluminum pot, there's no need for foil.

STEP TWO Add $1/2$ –1 c. baking soda, distributing it over and around the silver, then pour boiling water into the pot, completely submerging all the pieces.

STEP THREE Leave for 5 minutes—no longer than 10 minutes!—and rinse with warm water. Dry, then buff with a microfiber cloth. If tarnish remains, repeat soaking for 5 minutes.

STEP FOUR Apply a plain toothpaste (not a gel or paste with whitening chemicals) to the tarnished areas with a microfiber cloth. Wipe off and buff.

315 MAINTAIN THE TABLE

The dining table is the centerpiece of the room, so make sure you give it your complete attention. It doesn't take much effort to maintain a wooden table, yet a little neglect quickly degrades its presence.

CLEAR FINISH If your wooden dining set has a hard, transparent finish common to manufactured wooden furniture, it needs just a light dusting with a barely damp microfiber cloth. Wipe the legs in addition to the tabletop, especially in carved crevices where dust can settle—don't forget wooden chairs in addition to your table!

PAINTED FURNITURE For painted furniture, clean with a damp cloth. When stains and spills occur, use mild, soapy water and immediately dry.

316

CLEAN CHAIRS WITH SPINDLES

Dining chairs with spindles are notoriously a pain to clean. Spray them with the All-Purpose Cleaner (see tip 267) and let it sit for a few minutes before wiping well. Where the spindles attach to the chair, use compressed air to blast out crumbs and dirt. Then wrap a thin cloth around a butter knife or toothpick to scrape out anything left behind.

317 MIX IT UP

Changes in temperature and humidity can hurt wood furniture, so regularly rearrange the room to minimize the time one piece sits in adverse conditions. Avoid strong sunlight and heating sources such as radiators, space heaters, and fireplaces.

CHECKLISTS

The dining room is spare enough that an errant cobweb or a dusty tabletop screams, "I'm not ready!" So hold on to these checklists and always keep your dining room presentable for guests. Numbers refer to the general cleaning tips, so make sure to reference the appropriate supporting tips to address specific materials and circumstances.

DAILY
- ☐ Spot-clean spills and potential stains 002, 014
- ☐ Sweep or vacuum floors 039
- ☐ Spot-clean table linens 242
- ☐ Wash table linens 304
- ☐ Clear dining room table of clutter 301
- ☐ Wipe dining room table 315

WEEKLY
- ☐ Dust window treatments 019
- ☐ Dust doors and baseboards 023
- ☐ Clean switch plates 024
- ☐ Dust ceilings and walls 026
- ☐ Mop floors 040
- ☐ Vacuum carpets and area rugs 052, 054
- ☐ Dust sconces, lampshades, and chandeliers 065, 067, 069

MONTHLY
- ☐ Clean mirrors 018
- ☐ Clean window treatments 019
- ☐ Clean doorknobs 038
- ☐ Polish wooden furniture 277
- ☐ Clean light fixtures, chandeliers, and sconces 065, 067, 069

SEASONALLY (SPRING AND FALL)
- ☐ Wash windows 017
- ☐ Deep clean window treatments 019
- ☐ Wipe doors and baseboards 023
- ☐ Clean walls 026
- ☐ Deep clean lampshades 066
- ☐ Clean lamp bases 068
- ☐ Clean light fixtures, chandeliers, and sconces 067, 069, 070
- ☐ Polish silver 314
- ☐ Deep clean carpet and pad 303
- ☐ Clean underneath rugs 303
- ☐ Wash floor vents 303

318 CREATE A SLEEP SANCTUARY

Some cleaning habits are second nature by the time you're an adult: making the bed every day, putting dirty clothes in the hamper, returning to the closet the clothes you tried on and decided not to wear. It's tempting to leave one of those tasks undone when pressed for time. After all, only your nearest and dearest will see. But a clean and uncluttered bedroom is essential to creating a relaxing space where you can retreat. Take care of yourself by fostering a sanctuary in this intimate space.

319
PURGE YOUR CLOSET AND DRAWERS

It may take a little longer to sort through clothing that's in good shape, but it's a no-brainer to speedily to get rid of the following: old underwear, stockings with holes in them, orphan socks, and shoes that hurt your feet.

320
DESIGNATE A CLOTHING PURGATORY

If you don't feel motivated to put away clothes you wore for a short bit and plan on wearing again soon, you're not alone. Give yourself a break and keep it from spiraling out of control by specifying a zone for these items, like a few wall hooks or a stool in the corner of the bedroom.

321 CORRAL ESSENTIALS

Keep your bedroom tidy and easy to clean by gathering your nightstand clutter—hand cream, eyeglasses, chargers, remotes, books, water bottle, lip balm, etc.—in a tray or basket.

322 STORE EXTRAS UNDER YOUR BED

Tight on space? Use storage bins that slide under your bed or space-saver bags to store spare comforters, bulky blankets, or out-of-season clothing. Versions with wheels and handles make them even easier to retrieve.

323 TAKE IT EASY

Because the bedroom is not on show for guests, it's sometimes the last place we decorate. If that's the case with you, rethink your priorities. We spend one-third of our lives in the bed, sleeping to rejuvenate our bodies. Make your bedroom a spot that rejuvenates your spirit, too, giving you a boost to start the day and calming you in the evening. But consider long-term care commitments and less time-consuming alternatives. When the room is quick and easy to clean, you can spend your time on more important things.

WINDOW COVERINGS Instead of silk draperies, consider the attractive options in easy-to-clean indoor/outdoor fabric or no drapes at all. Plantation shutters are stylish and easy to clean.

FLOORS Do you really need carpeting, or would hardwood floors allow you to capture more of the dust that's hiding in your room?

BEDDING Look for bed skirts, decorative pillows, and duvet covers in washable fabrics. White bedding looks great, and tossing it in the wash once a week keeps it clean.

324 LAUNDER SHEETS WEEKLY

Wash your sheets once a week. It doesn't take much time, and the payoff comes when you slide into a fresh, spotless cocoon at night. Use warm water, wash colors separately, and use a low-heat drying cycle. Dryer heat will permanently set a stain, so make sure to treat all stains (see tip 242) before bed linens go into the dryer.

325 LINE-DRY YOUR SHEETS

What once was customary, then fell out of practice, is now coming back. People are choosing to line-dry their laundry again for a myriad of reasons, including economical and environmental. If you haven't felt the freshness of sheets that have been dried in the sun, it's worth the experience. Drape your newly washed sheet in half over your clothesline and secure it with clothespins about 1 ft. apart. Make sure your clothesline is high enough that the wet sheet won't weigh it down too far toward the ground. If you don't have room outside, you can air-dry your sheets indoors by hanging them over your shower curtain rod or a couple of drying racks and rotating them every few hours.

326 PROTECT PILLOWS

A zippered pillow protector fits snugly over the pillow; the pillowcase goes on top of it. This extra layer prevents natural skin oil and lotions from staining the pillow, extending its useful life. But more importantly, a cover protects your family from dust mites and other allergens inside the pillow. Wash it monthly as you would a pillowcase, without bleach or fabric softener. Put it in the dryer on a low-heat setting, but do not iron.

327 SOFTEN BEDDING

Instead of using commercial fabric softeners that include harmful chemicals, simply pour $1/2$ c. white vinegar in the fabric softener dispenser with each wash. Vinegar is a natural softening agent and removes soap residue from the sheets.

328 CASE OUT PILLOWS

It's a good idea to have extra pillowcases on hand in case they need laundering more than once a week. Makeup and face lotions often soil a pillowcase. Replace it right away and treat the stain. If you have teens in the house, it's a good idea to give them a fresh pillowcase frequently to stave off acne breakouts.

329 MINIMIZE WRINKLES

Take sheets out of the dryer before they are completely dry and you'll have fewer wrinkles. Make the bed, smoothing out wrinkles with your hand, and let the sheets finish air-drying before you put a cover over them.

330 CARE FOR PILLOWS

You may regularly wash your pillowcases, but what about the pillows themselves? Bedroom pillows need a thorough wash twice a year. Most synthetic and down pillows are machine-washable, but double-check the care tag.

STEP ONE Strip off any cases, sham covers, protectors, and allergy covers, and wash those separately.

STEP TWO Wash two pillows at a time to balance the load in the machine, using liquid detergent and warm water. Program the machine to go through two rinse cycles to remove as much soap as possible.

STEP THREE Transfer pillows to the dryer and set it on the air cycle for down or a low-heat setting for synthetics. Add a couple of wool dryer balls to fluff the pillows, separate the down, and deter clumps.

331 REVITALIZE MEMORY FOAM

Pillows made from memory foam are becoming increasingly popular due to their ability to create a customized fit while still providing support. But this material requires special care.

DUNK Remove the cover from the pillow and submerge it in a sink or tub filled with warm water.

MIX Add 1 tbsp. mild liquid laundry detergent to the water, and swirl and squeeze the pillow to let the water and soap work their way through.

RINSE Drain the soapy water and refill the sink with cool water. Swirl and squeeze the pillow—replacing the water as necessary—until you are confident there is no more soap in the pillow.

DRY Never put memory foam in the dryer. Instead, gently press water out and allow it to completely air-dry on a white towel.

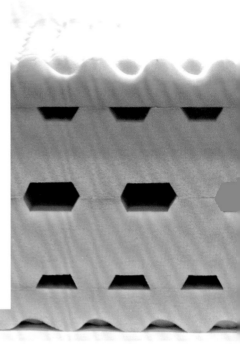

332 SHIELD YOUR COMFORTER

Don't wash a comforter more often than twice a year. Washing too frequently will compact the fill, diminishing its capacity for warmth. It's the air trapped within a light, fluffy filling that provides the insulation to keep your body heat from escaping into the room. Protect the comforter from body oils by encasing it in fabric. An attractive duvet cover can be washed monthly, saving the comforter for a seasonal cleaning.

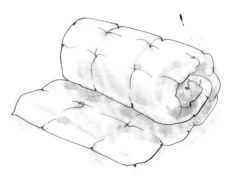

333 USE CLIPS

If you struggle keeping your comforter inside your duvet cover or your sheets on your bed, give bedding clips a try. They grab the corners of your bedding and help keep everything in place.

334 CLEAN THE COMFORTER

Before you wash a comforter or duvet, read the care tag attached to one of the corners and follow the directions. Check for stains, tears, and holes that need repair. Spot-clean according to the guidelines in the laundry-stains list (see tip 242), but push the filling aside when treating stains. And consider your washer's capacity for a king- or queen-sized comforter; you may need to go to a laundromat for larger-capacity washers, or to a dry cleaner.

DOWN, COTTON, OR SYNTHETIC Wash comforters filled with these materials on the delicate cycle with warm or cold water and a mild detergent. Distribute the comforter evenly in the machine and use an extra rinse cycle. Dry on the fluff setting with wool dryer balls, and periodically stop the dryer to fluff and distribute the filler. You could also air-dry the comforter, fluffing and distributing the fill as it dries.

WOOL Hand-wash wool-filled comforters. Fill the bathtub with warm, soapy water and gently press the comforter up and down in the water. Rinse thoroughly, repeating until the water runs clear. Gently press excess water from the comforter and hang outside to dry. Before hand-washing, consider the risk of felting and the weight when wet. You may prefer to dry-clean it.

SILK There's really no way around it: A silk-filled comforter must be dry-cleaned to avoid damage.

335   FRESHEN A MATTRESS

Even though you can't wash your mattress, you can regularly clean it. And you should. Follow the suggestions below to make it more comfortable for sleep and to help it last as long as possible.

STEP ONE Strip the bed and let the mattress air out for an hour or two.

STEP TWO Vacuum the mattress with the upholstery and crevice attachments. Be meticulous about covering the entire surface and getting into the seams: The vacuum will suction up dust mites if you're thorough.

STEP THREE Spot-clean stains, adapting guidelines for removing laundry stains (see tip 242) when appropriate. When in doubt, follow the directions for cleaning upholstery (see tip 266). Be careful not to saturate the mattress, and let it completely air-dry.

STEP FOUR Deodorize the mattress by shaking out an entire box of baking soda over its surface. Let the baking soda sit for as long as you can to let it neutralize all odors, and then vacuum it up. The best time for you to freshen up your mattress is before you leave for vacation.

336
WASH THE MATTRESS PAD

Use a mattress pad to prolong the life of your mattress by screening it from accidental spills and from natural skin oils and perspiration that would otherwise yellow the mattress. If there's no care tag, follow these general directions.

COTTON Spot-treat stains first, machine-wash with warm water, and dry on a low-heat setting.

FOAM Because a washing machine is too hard on foam mattress pads, spot-clean instead if you see a stain. Otherwise, just vacuum both sides. If you feel that an overall cleaning is warranted, make a spray of 1 part mild soap to 2 parts water and spray it on the pad. Let it sit for 30 minutes, then thoroughly rinse in the shower or tub. Gently squeeze out the water and air-dry, flipping the pad as needed to completely dry.

VINYL AND PLASTIC Spot-clean any stains and vacuum the front and back. Put the pad in the washer using warm or cold water with mild detergent. Dry on the air-fluff cycle only, adding wool dryer balls to speed drying. If it is not completely dry when the cycle ends, leave it out to air-dry with the vinyl or plastic side up first, then turn it over to dry the fabric side.

EGG CRATE Spot-clean and vacuum both sides, then spray with a solution of 1 part mild soap to 2 parts water. Rinse in a tub or shower and carefully squeeze out excess water so as not to rip the egg crate. Air-dry, flipping the pad as needed to dry it completely.

337 TREAT CURTAINS AND BED SKIRTS

In addition to the necessary bed fittings, you may enjoy dressing your bed with a bed skirt, decorative pillows, or bed curtains. All of these enhance the bed, but are harder to categorize by cleaning methods. Read the attached care tag for special handling, but follow these general care instructions.

BED SKIRTS Silk and wool skirts must be dry-cleaned, but cotton and linen skirts can be machine-washed, particularly if they are white. With colors or patterns, check for colorfastness by wetting a small, inconspicuous corner and patting the spot with a white cotton washcloth to look for color bleeding. If there is none, machine-wash in cold water. If the color bleeds, dry-clean it. Dry on a medium- or low-heat setting, remove while still damp, and immediately iron.

DECORATIVE PILLOWS Pillows with beading and embroidery, especially on velvet, accumulate dust over time. Your best bet may be canned air, which is sold at office supply stores. Start in an area without beading or heavy embroidery to be certain the air pressure won't push the beads off. You can also try vacuuming on low suction, but first stretch hosiery over the dust-brush attachment to prevent snagging of any threads.

BED CURTAINS Treat curtains and canopies as you would window draperies, taking them down seasonally for cleaning (see tip 022). If they are silk, wool, or lined draperies, dry-cleaning is safer.

338 DIFFUSE CALMING SCENTS

Wind down at night with an essential oil diffuser. Many people are turning toward diffusers as a more natural alternative to scented candles. Available in a variety of types that look like stylish décor, diffusers disperse aromatic essential oils into the air to scent a room. Chamomile and lavender are splendid scents for relaxation.

CLEAN YOUR DIFFUSER

First, unplug the diffuser. Then put a splash of white vinegar and some water in the bottom of your empty diffuser. Let it sit while you wash the diffuser lid in your sink with regular dish soap and water. Dump out the vinegar water and rinse it really well so there's not any residue. Be careful to avoid getting any electrical elements wet. Use a cotton swab to clean any hard-to-reach spots. Wipe dry.

339 SCENT WITH LAVENDER

Using lavender essential oil is a great bedtime routine. Mist it over pillows and linens; it's easy to make and creates a calming atmosphere.

LAVENDER ROOM SPRAY

1 $\frac{1}{2}$ oz. rubbing alcohol

1 $\frac{1}{2}$ oz. water

30 drops lavender essential oil

Mix all ingredients in a 4-oz. spray bottle. Shake well before each use.

340

DON'T FORGET THE BED FRAME

We're so good about cleaning sheets and pillowcases, but the frame—be it a wood tester, an upholstered headboard, a metal canopy, or a modern platform—gets taken for granted. Dust monthly with a damp microfiber cloth to avoid buildup.

341 ADDRESS THE DRESSER

Drawers may store clean clothes, but they still need to be seasonally cleaned and decluttered. Empty drawers and cabinets so you can thoroughly vacuum all interior spaces with a dust-brush attachment, then wipe with a soft cloth or sponge dampened with the All-Purpose Cleaner (see tip 267), using a toothbrush to loosen debris around the edges and corners. Wipe again with a cloth dampened with water to remove any trace of the cleaner, then let them completely dry before returning the contents.

342 REMOVE TARNISH FROM HANDLES

Whether you're dealing with a family heirloom or a DIY job, dull and discolored dresser hardware can be a downer. Depending on the shape they're in, you may need to try some or all of the following steps. After removing the handles, first try soaking them overnight in a mixture of warm water and vinegar. Next, make a paste of equal parts salt, vinegar, and flour to scrub on the handles with a toothbrush. If neither of those did the job, try cleaning them with plain white toothpaste.

343 TACKLE A CEILING FAN

Clean fans twice a year, spreading a drop cloth or large sheet on the floor first and wearing safety glasses to protect your eyes from falling dust. It's easier to reach all the parts using a ladder, although you may be able to do so with a microfiber wand. Spray the All-Purpose Cleaner (see tip 267) on a microfiber cloth or wand, and wipe each blade, top and bottom. Dust the motor housing as well as the downrod. Chances are you'll need to rinse the cloth and reapply spray, or replace cloths as they become too dirty to pick up more dust.

 344 CAPTURE DUST WITH A PILLOWCASE

Between more thorough cleanings, use a pillowcase to wipe down your ceiling fan. Slip it over each fan blade, one at a time, and wipe as you pull it off. The pillowcase will capture the dust. Then you can shake it outside and launder as normal.

345 CLEAN A FABRIC HEADBOARD

The best way to remove spots on a fabric headboard is with a little dish soap, although it's essential that you test the method on a discreet spot, especially if the fabric is decorative and may not be colorfast. A good testing spot is on the back of the headboard or at a level low enough not to show above the mattress.

SUDS Create a thick sudsy foam by whipping up equal parts dishwashing liquid and water. Apply the foam to the spot or stain.

RUB Gently work the foam into the stain with your fingertips so as not to strain the fabric. Let it sit for 5 minutes.

REMOVE Rinse a sponge with water and apply water to the stain to remove the soapy foam. Blot it dry with a microfiber cloth. You may have to repeat on stubborn stains.

DRY Soak up as much moisture as you can with a microfiber cloth. Let it air-dry completely.

346 MAINTAIN A HUMIDIFIER

It's important to change the water every day and regularly inspect the unit. Mold and mildew are always a concern with a humidifier, so clean and disinfect it once a week. Refer to the owner's manual for cleaning instructions specific to your device, but otherwise follow these general guidelines to keep a clean machine.

STEP ONE Drain all water from the tank. Refill it with cold water and add 1 tsp. vinegar per gallon of water. Let it soak for 30 minutes while the vinegar kills mold and bacteria.

STEP TWO Take the machine apart to access the filter, water reservoir, and any other removable parts. Thoroughly rinse the filter with nothing but cold water; vinegar and soap may damage a filter.

STEP THREE Pour white vinegar into the water reservoir in the base of the unit, right up to the fill line, and let it soak for 30 minutes.

Put other loose parts into a bowl or bucket of white vinegar for 30 minutes.

STEP FOUR Scrub the base and all loose parts—except for the filter—with a tooth-brush, or any tool that came with the humidi-fier. Pay attention to mineral deposits and dis-colored areas. Drain the vinegar, rinse all parts, and let them air-dry.

STEP FIVE Reassemble your humidifier and then refill the tank with clean water. Remem-ber, it's important to change the water in the tank every day.

347 HUNT FOR BUNNIES

Dust bunnies live in spots that we don't see regularly, so you'll need to seek them out. Under the bed is one of their favorite hiding places. Make a habit of using your microfiber wand to sweep under the bed, bedside table, and chest of drawers once a week.

348 CLEAN CLOSETS

An annual scrubbing of closets is crucial. They're dark and often crowded with lots of places for dust bunnies, cobwebs, and critters to hide. Take everything out of the closet—down to the bare walls and floors—and vacuum the floors, walls, and ceiling using the crevice and dust-brush attachments to get into corners and high spots. Wash every surface and corner with the Nonabrasive Vinegar Cleaner (see tip 267), which will not only loosen dirt but also kill moth eggs so small that you can't see them. Let the space air-dry before returning clothes, shoes, and boxes to the closet.

349 COLLECT DONATIONS

Find a spot in your closet or bedroom (even under the bed would work) to stash a box or bag of clothes to be donated. Whenever you feel ready to let something go, put it in there right away. When the box or bag is filled, list everything on Facebook Marketplace or bring the items to your favorite shelter or donation spot.

350

USE A FREESTANDING CLOTHING RACK

Tiny closet? A slim hanging rack can serve as the perfect place for storing overflow items such as your outfits for the week or your coats and accessories. Look for a design that maximizes its footprint with a bottom shelf.

351 SUCK UP SMELLS

Naturally absorb odors in stinky spaces such as shoe baskets with charcoal air-purifying bags. They "recharge" in the sunlight, so you can reuse them again and again.

352 MAKE SPACE

Make the switch to velvet clothes hangers. They take up a fraction of the space that a hodgepodge of plastic, wire, and wooden hangers would, and they keep a tight grip on your clothes. Even spaghetti straps stay on!

353 MAKE LAVENDER SACHETS

Lavender is a natural moth repellent, so lavender sachets are the perfect natural alternative to toxic mothballs. Not only are they simple to make, they also look and smell lovely. Follow these steps to create two sachets that you can place in your closet or tuck into drawers.

STEP ONE Cut a vintage handkerchief into four even squares, and sew two pieces of the fabric together, inside out, leaving a couple of inches at the top.

STEP TWO Flip the fabric right side out and fill the sachets half full with dried lavender buds.

STEP THREE Carefully sew the remaining end closed, either with a basic edge or decorative flap. Repeat with the remaining fabric. Enjoy your clothes while deterring moths.

STEP FOUR Remember to replace the lavender if the fragrance fades so you have year-round protection from new moth eggs. If you can't smell the lavender anymore, neither can they!

354 PROTECT FABRICS WITH CEDAR

Red cedar has been used for many generations to ward off moths. If lavender is too floral for your tastes, cedar is a great alternative. Some entire closets and clothes-storing chests are lined or built from cedar, but you can also find them as small balls or as hanging blocks. As with lavender, it's the scent of cedar that deters moths, so it's important to renew the scent when it wanes. A light sanding will do the trick, plus a coat of cedar oil, sold in many home supply stores.

355 CHASE THE MOTHS

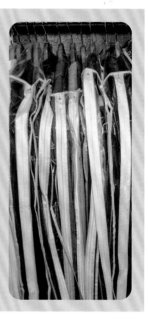

It takes only one noticeable moth hole in a favorite skirt to make moth prevention a priority. The moths themselves don't harm fabrics; it's their larvae that feed on natural fibers like wool, silk, and feathers. Every spring—before you put winter clothes and wool blankets away—follow these easy steps to protect against moth holes.

CLEAN You can get rid of any hard-to-see larvae or eggs by doing a full cleaning of your closet (see tip 348), including those hard-to-reach shelves and any boxes of shoes that you have seldom worn.

LAUNDER Dry-clean or wash all winter clothes before storing them. It's often dirty clothes with perspiration, perfume scents, and food stains that attract moths in the first place.

PROTECT Store clothing in airtight plastic boxes or bags over the summer. Use packing tape to seal the lids, and block even the tiniest air space where a moth could possibly enter and lay eggs.

356 DESTROY DUST MITES

Dust mites are rarely a big issue if you regularly wash your sheets and clean your bedroom. But to be on the safe side, make sure you're doing the following to chase the mites away.

HEAT Wash bedsheets, mattress covers, pillows, and pillow covers in water heated to at least 130 degrees Fahrenheit (54 degrees Celsius) and dry on high heat.

REPLACE Buy new comforters and pillows every 2 years.

PROTECT Use hypoallergenic, dust mite–averse pillow and mattress covers. Plastic is the best to prevent mites.

FILTER Vacuum often, and be sure your vacuum has a high-efficiency particulate air (HEPA) filter.

DRY Maintain low humidity levels in the house; dust mites thrive in high humidity.

RESTRAIN Keep pets out of the bedroom. Dust mites love pet dander.

CHILL Set the thermostat at 70 degrees Fahrenheit (21 degrees Celsius) or less.

357 ELIMINATE LICE

It's not the end of the world if you get word that your child has lice. It's a common rite of passage, so don't panic, but do act quickly and efficiently. Ask your pediatrician for expert recommendations on how to eliminate lice on the head, then focus on these steps to prevent them from infesting the house.

STEP ONE Identify everything that may have come in contact with the head—bedding, stuffed animals, hairbrush, comb, hats, headsets, coats, clothes.

STEP TWO Wash all the bedding and clothing in the washing machine at high heat for an extended cycle, even if it requires multiple loads. Soak hairbrushes and hair accessories for an hour in water heated to at least 130 degrees Fahrenheit (54 degrees Celsius). Gather nonwashables, such as headphones and delicate hats, seal in a plastic bag, and put the bag in the freezer for 24 hours.

STEP THREE For pieces too large to go in the washer or freezer, put them in an airtight plastic bag and leave it sealed for 2 weeks to suffocate the lice.

STEP FOUR Vacuum all surfaces, including mattresses, rugs, and carpets.

STEP FIVE Check everyone's head every day until the lice are gone, following your doctor's orders, and once a week for 1 month afterward to make sure no more eggs have hatched.

BEDROOM

CHECKLISTS

Start your day off on the right foot by implementing a cleaning routine to give your bedroom the care it deserves. If you maintain a certain level of order and cleanliness, you'll have more time to enjoy the things that matter most. A little effort each day enables you to enjoy a relaxing evening and wake up to a stress-free morning. Numbers refer to the general cleaning tips, so make sure to reference the appropriate supporting tips to address specific materials and circumstances.

DAILY

- ☐ Spot-clean spills and potential stains 002, 014
- ☐ Sweep or vacuum floors 039
- ☐ Put dirty clothes in hamper 318
- ☐ Declutter dresser and nightstand 341

WEEKLY

- ☐ Dust window treatments 019
- ☐ Dust doors and baseboards 023
- ☐ Clean switch plates 024
- ☐ Dust ceilings and walls 026
- ☐ Vacuum carpets and area rugs 052, 054
- ☐ Dust lamps and lampshades 065
- ☐ Wipe wooden furniture 278
- ☐ Wash bed linens 324
- ☐ Disinfect humidifier 346
- ☐ Dust under furniture 347

MONTHLY

- ☐ Clean mirrors 018
- ☐ Clean window treatments 019
- ☐ Wash trash cans 037
- ☐ Clean doorknobs 038
- ☐ Polish wooden furniture 277
- ☐ Wash pillow covers 326
- ☐ Wash comforter cover 332
- ☐ Vacuum mattress 335
- ☐ Wash mattress pad 336
- ☐ Dust bed frame 340

SEASONALLY (SPRING AND FALL)

- ☐ Wash windows 017
- ☐ Deep clean window treatments 019
- ☐ Wipe doors and baseboards 023
- ☐ Deep clean ceilings and walls 026
- ☐ Deep clean lampshades 066
- ☐ Clean lamp bases and sconces 067, 068
- ☐ Clean ceiling fixtures 070
- ☐ Wash pillows and comforters 330, 334
- ☐ Clean mattress 335
- ☐ Treat bed curtains and skirts 337
- ☐ Clean dresser drawers 341
- ☐ Clean ceiling fan 343
- ☐ Clean closet 348
- ☐ Clean and store winter clothing 355

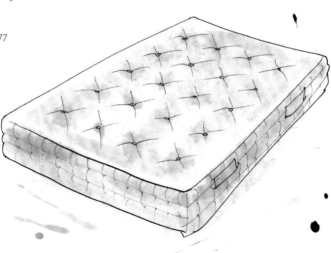

358 GET ORGANIZED

A home office is a much-needed space to pay bills, organize tax-related documents, keep up with the school calendar, and perhaps do homework. But it has to be clean and orderly for everyone to work efficiently. A messy workspace prevents you from getting your tasks done. Address the clutter, and then cleaning your office space will be easy, helping you maintain the ideal work-life balance.

359 MAKE AN OFFICE ANYWHERE

Short on space or don't have a dedicated home office? Carve out a creative work-from-home space with a wall-mounted, fold-down desk or by sneaking a desktop into a closet or unused corner.

360 RECYCLE YOUR E-WASTE

Getting a new laptop or cell phone is exciting, but what should you do with your old version? Don't let it end up in a landfill. Find a place for them through a service like the Recycle Locator on the Consumer Technology Association's website. The Environmental Protection Agency also lists companies such as Staples and Best Buy that offer electronics donation and recycling.

361 TRY WHITE NOISE FOR PRIVACY

Working from home in an apartment you share with roommates? Block out distracting conversations and street noise with a portable sound machine.

QUICK TIP

GRAB CRUMBS WITH A STICKY NOTE

Slide the adhesive side of a sticky note in the nooks and crannies of your keyboard to easily snatch rogue crumbs or dust.

CLEAN A COMPUTER

It's inevitable that a computer will begin to show a smudged screen, dirty keyboard, and dusty vents. Not only is that uninviting to work on, but accumulated dust can interfere with performance. Always check the owner's manual for specific care requirements before cleaning. It takes only a few minutes once a week to keep your computer looking new.

As with all electronics, remember that even a stray drop of water can prove fatal, so keep cleaning fluids at a safe distance to avoid spills, and make sure that all cleaning cloths are only slightly damp—always tightly squeeze as much moisture as possible out of the cleaning cloth to avoid drips or accumulated moisture. And let your electronics sit unused for a few hours after cleaning to make sure even trace amounts of moisture have dried up.

SCREEN A dry microfiber cloth will pick up any dust on the screen. Put the least amount of water possible in a corner of the cloth to wipe away fingerprints or smudges, but be careful not to put any pressure on the screen itself.

KEYBOARD Spray compressed air in bursts to blow away dust hiding in crevices—you may want to unplug the keyboard and do this outside if you expect a lot of debris. If you haven't used a can of compressed air before, practice and use the can's extension wand, which will help your precision. Be wary of holding the can too close to the keyboard, as it will produce condensation that's harmful to the keyboard's electronics.

After loosening any dust with the compressed air, turn the keyboard upside down and gently shake it to dislodge debris. For dirt and grime on the keys or keyboard frame, wipe with a cloth just moistened with an alcohol solution of 1 part rubbing alcohol to 1 part water. Dip a cotton swab in the alcohol solution and clean between each key. Wipe again with a dry cloth.

MOUSE Unplug the mouse from your computer and remove any batteries. Clean the mouse's exterior with a barely damp microfiber cloth and dry with a second cloth. Don't remove the scroll wheel; instead, turn the mouse upside down and roll the wheel to spin out dust.

For an optical mouse, very gently wipe the lens with a cotton swab dampened with the alcohol solution. Use a cloth dampened with the same alcohol solution to clean the rubber feet on the bottom to ensure that the mouse glides easily.

To clean a mouse with a rolling ball, turn it over and remove the bottom panel to release the ball. Clean the ball with a microfiber cloth dampened with the alcohol solution, let it dry, then put the mouse back together. Refer to the owner's manual for any other internal cleaning instructions.

CASE Turn the computer off and unplug it. Wipe the exterior desktop case or laptop casing with a microfiber cloth slightly dampened with mild, soapy water. A cotton swab dipped in the soapy water cleans vents and tight corners. Repeat, wiping the outside again with a clean, damp cloth to remove any remaining soap, and then dry with a clean cloth.

CORDS Anything you can do to keep the room air dust free helps your computer, so wipe the entire cord and plug with a microfiber cloth, too.

ACCESSORIES Items such as a mouse pad, keyboard pad, or desk blotter can also accumulate dust or grime, especially from the oils in your skin. Give them a thorough wipedown with the All-Purpose Cleaner (see tip 267) and let them dry fully before putting back into place.

363 CLEAR COMPUTER CLUTTER

Delete unnecessary files and programs on your computer and organize important ones. Merge duplicate files. Erase downloads. Empty the trash. Delete unused bookmarks. While you're at it, set a new desktop wallpaper. Next, do the same to your phone and tablet.

364 CREATE A HOME BINDER

While going paperless is a great goal for many areas, it's helpful to keep hard copies of some things all in one place. Organize the essential paperwork for your home in a binder. Keeping contracts, receipts, manuals, repair notes, and warranties in one place makes it easy to find contact information for work you've had done and is a wonderful resource to pass along to any future owners of your home.

365 ORGANIZE CORDS

Tangled cords and loose chargers are annoying and look messy. Get them under control by experimenting with these solutions.

CHARGING STATIONS Docks for charging multiple devices at once.

CABLE CLIPS These clips have adhesive backs and rubbery fingers that hold cords in place.

VELCRO CABLE TIES Wrap snugly around grouped cords and furniture legs.

CABLE SLEEVES Fabric covers that gather and hide bundled cords.

CABLE ORGANIZER BOX Covers several plugs or hides an entire power strip.

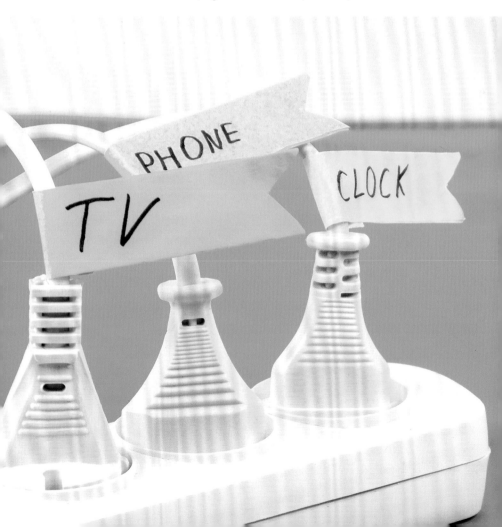

CHECKLISTS

Whether you're in the office every day or just evenings, when you take care of household bills and chores, the office should be organized and stress free. Plan your cleaning activities so they become a ritual, part of the day-to-day process that brings out the best in you! Numbers refer to the general cleaning tips, so make sure to reference the appropriate supporting tips to address specific materials and circumstances.

DAILY
- [ ] Spot-clean spills and potential stains 002, 014
- [ ] Sweep or vacuum floors 039

WEEKLY
- [ ] Dust window treatments 019
- [ ] Dust doors and baseboards 023
- [ ] Clean switch plates 024
- [ ] Dust ceilings and walls 026
- [ ] Vacuum carpets and area rugs 052, 054
- [ ] Dust lampshades and chandeliers 065, 069
- [ ] Wipe wooden furniture 278
- [ ] Clean computer 362
- [ ] Empty trash can

MONTHLY
- [ ] Clean mirrors 018
- [ ] Clean window treatments 019
- [ ] Wash trash cans 037
- [ ] Clean doorknobs 038
- [ ] Polish wooden furniture 277
- [ ] Dust books and bookshelves 293, 294
- [ ] Vacuum office chair

SEASONALLY (SPRING AND FALL)
- [ ] Wash windows 017
- [ ] Deep clean window treatments 019
- [ ] Wipe doors and baseboards 023
- [ ] Clean walls 026
- [ ] Deep clean lampshades 066
- [ ] Clean lamp bases and sconces 067, 068
- [ ] Clean fixtures 070
- [ ] Clear computer clutter 363
- [ ] Organize cords 365

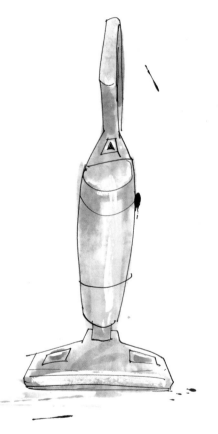

CLEANING CHECKLISTS

DAILY

Use this master checklist of daily cleaning suggestions to create a routine that works for you. You can customize the list to create a cleaning system that works for your home and your schedule. You'll be amazed at the difference you can make by investing just a few extra minutes each morning and evening!

KITCHEN
- ☐ Sweep or vacuum floors 039
- ☐ Wipe counters and tables 131
- ☐ Wipe stovetop 101
- ☐ Wash dishes 107
- ☐ Load and run dishwasher 115
- ☐ Wipe dishwasher exterior 114
- ☐ Clean sink 123
- ☐ Wipe faucets 128
- ☐ Clean minor appliances 100, 140, 141, 145, 146, 147
- ☐ Put out new dish towels 084

BATHROOM
- ☐ Sweep or vacuum floors 039
- ☐ Wipe faucets 163
- ☐ Wipe sinks and counters 163
- ☐ Squeegee shower 163
- ☐ Rinse bathtub 163
- ☐ Rinse and dry whirlpool 163
- ☐ Swish toilets 217

LAUNDRY
- ☐ Sweep or vacuum floors 039
- ☐ Declutter laundry room 227
- ☐ Spot-treat stains 242
- ☐ Wash clothes 227
- ☐ Dry clothes 253
- ☐ Clean lint filter 255

LIVING ROOM
- ☐ Spot-clean spills and potential stains 002, 014, 268, 274
- ☐ Straighten throw pillows 276
- ☐ Sweep or vacuum floors 039

DINING AREA
- ☐ Spot-clean spills and potential stains 002, 014
- ☐ Sweep or vacuum floors 039
- ☐ Spot-clean table linens 242
- ☐ Wash table linens 304
- ☐ Clear dining room table of clutter 301
- ☐ Wipe dining room table 315

BEDROOM
- ☐ Spot-clean spills and potential stains 002, 014
- ☐ Sweep or vacuum floors 039
- ☐ Put dirty clothes in hamper 318
- ☐ Declutter dresser and nightstand 341

OFFICE
- ☐ Spot-clean spills and potential stains 002, 014
- ☐ Sweep or vacuum floors 039

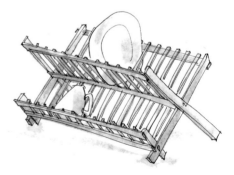

WEEKLY

Set aside a few hours each weekend to keep your home looking great! If you prefer to reserve weekends for family and friends, designate some time during the weekdays to accomplish these tasks. That way you'll have the satisfaction that comes with a job well done as you relax and recharge. You've earned it!

KITCHEN
- [ ] Dust window treatments 019
- [ ] Dust doors and baseboards 023
- [ ] Clean switch plates 024
- [ ] Dust ceilings and walls 026
- [ ] Mop floors 040
- [ ] Dust lampshades and chandeliers 065, 069
- [ ] Clean refrigerator interior and exterior 086
- [ ] Clean stovetop 101
- [ ] Clean disposal 125
- [ ] Wipe cabinet doors 158
- [ ] Disinfect handles and knobs 162

BATHROOM
- [ ] Clean mirrors 018
- [ ] Dust window treatments 019
- [ ] Dust doors and baseboards 023
- [ ] Clean switch plates 024
- [ ] Dust ceilings and walls 026
- [ ] Mop floors 040
- [ ] Freshen air 171
- [ ] Scrub shower 180
- [ ] Deep clean tub 187
- [ ] Wash towels, bath mats, and bathrobes 193, 195, 196
- [ ] Clean sink 197
- [ ] Wash makeup and hairbrushes 213, 216
- [ ] Wash canisters, glasses, and soap dishes 215
- [ ] Wipe down toilet exterior and tank 217
- [ ] Clean toilet brush 219

LAUNDRY
- [ ] Dust window treatments 019
- [ ] Dust doors and baseboards 023
- [ ] Clean switch plates 024
- [ ] Dust ceilings and walls 026
- [ ] Mop floors 040
- [ ] Wipe down washer and dryer

LIVING ROOM
- [ ] Dust window treatments 019
- [ ] Dust doors and baseboards 023
- [ ] Clean switch plates 024
- [ ] Dust ceilings and walls 026
- [ ] Vacuum carpets and area rugs 052, 054
- [ ] Dust lampshades and chandeliers 065, 069
- [ ] Tend the Fireplace 281, 282, 283, 285, 286, 287, 288
- [ ] Wipe wooden furniture 278
- [ ] Dust TV 290
- [ ] Clean remote controls 292

DINING AREA
- [ ] Dust window treatments 019
- [ ] Dust doors and baseboards 023
- [ ] Clean switch plates 024
- [ ] Dust ceilings and walls 026
- [ ] Mop floors 040
- [ ] Vacuum carpets and area rugs 052, 054
- [ ] Dust sconces, lampshades, and chandeliers 065, 067, 069

BEDROOM
- [ ] Dust window treatments 019
- [ ] Dust doors and baseboards 023
- [ ] Clean switch plates 024
- [ ] Dust ceilings and walls 026
- [ ] Vacuum carpets and area rugs 052, 054
- [ ] Dust lamps and lampshades 065
- [ ] Wipe wooden furniture 278
- [ ] Wash bed linens 324
- [ ] Dust under furniture 347
- [ ] Disinfect humidifier 346

OFFICE
- [ ] Dust window treatments 019
- [ ] Dust doors and baseboards 023
- [ ] Clean switch plates 024
- [ ] Dust ceilings and walls 026
- [ ] Vacuum carpets and area rugs 052, 054
- [ ] Dust lampshades and chandeliers 065, 069
- [ ] Wipe wooden furniture 278
- [ ] Clean computer 362
- [ ] Empty trash can 037

MONTHLY

The whole house needs a thorough cleaning once a month to freshen it up from everyday wear. Use this list to help stay on top of the infrequent and deep cleaning tasks that require your attention.

KITCHEN
- ☐ Clean window treatments 019
- ☐ Wash trash cans 037
- ☐ Clean doorknobs 038
- ☐ Steam clean microwave 100
- ☐ Sanitize dishwasher interior 119
- ☐ Deep clean disposal 125
- ☐ Deep clean minor appliances 100, 140, 141, 145, 146, 147
- ☐ Clean knobs 162

BATHROOM
- ☐ Clean window treatments 019
- ☐ Wash trash cans 037
- ☐ Sanitize whirlpool tub 190
- ☐ Clear drains 191
- ☐ Clean tub exterior 188
- ☐ Deep clean toilet bowl and tank 217
- ☐ Remove minerals from toilet 218

LAUNDRY
- ☐ Clean window treatments 019
- ☐ Wash trash cans 037
- ☐ Clean doorknobs 038
- ☐ Clean washer 246, 249, 250
- ☐ Clean sink 197
- ☐ Sweep and mop behind washer and dryer 254

LIVING ROOM
- ☐ Clean mirrors 018
- ☐ Clean window treatments 019
- ☐ Wash trash cans 037
- ☐ Clean doorknobs 038
- ☐ Vacuum upholstered furniture 265
- ☐ Clean leather upholstery 273
- ☐ Polish wooden furniture 277
- ☐ Dust and clean speakers 291
- ☐ Dust books and bookshelves 293, 294

DINING AREA
- ☐ Clean mirrors 018
- ☐ Clean window treatments 019
- ☐ Clean doorknobs 038
- ☐ Clean light fixtures, chandeliers, and sconces 065, 067, 069
- ☐ Polish wooden furniture 277

BEDROOM
- ☐ Clean mirrors 018
- ☐ Clean window treatments 019
- ☐ Wash trash cans 037
- ☐ Clean doorknobs 038
- ☐ Polish wooden furniture 277
- ☐ Wash pillow covers 326
- ☐ Wash comforter cover 332
- ☐ Vacuum mattress 335
- ☐ Wash mattress pad 336
- ☐ Dust bed frame 340

OFFICE
- ☐ Clean mirrors 018
- ☐ Clean window treatments 019
- ☐ Wash trash cans 037
- ☐ Clean doorknobs 038
- ☐ Dust window treatments 019
- ☐ Polish wooden furniture 277
- ☐ Dust books and bookshelves 293, 294
- ☐ Vacuum office chair

SEASONALLY

Every spring and fall, plan for a thorough seasonal cleaning that prepares your household for the next 6 months. Tackle these big events as a whole family and everyone will feel the satisfaction of a team effort.

KITCHEN

- ☐ Wash windows 017
- ☐ Deep clean window treatments 019
- ☐ Wipe doors and baseboards 023
- ☐ Clean walls 026
- ☐ Clean light fixtures, chandeliers, and sconces 067, 069, 070
- ☐ Deep clean refrigerator and freezer 086
- ☐ Replace liners 160
- ☐ Clean condenser coils 091
- ☐ Deep clean stove and oven 096
- ☐ Clean vent hood and filter 106
- ☐ Deep clean dishwasher and filter 120
- ☐ Scour disposal 126
- ☐ Clean knife block 143
- ☐ Clean out cabinets and drawers 153
- ☐ Clean inside cabinets and drawers 153
- ☐ Reseal countertops 131

BATHROOM

- ☐ Wash windows 017
- ☐ Deep clean window treatments 019
- ☐ Wipe doors and baseboards 023
- ☐ Clean walls 026
- ☐ Clean sconces and light fixtures 067, 070
- ☐ Purge medicine cabinet 174
- ☐ Wash shower curtain 180
- ☐ Clean showerhead 183
- ☐ Clean vent 184
- ☐ Clean grout 185
- ☐ Clean shelves, drawers, and cabinets 200
- ☐ Clean makeup drawer 202
- ☐ Clean jewelry box 203
- ☐ Restock bathroom caddy 165

LAUNDRY

- ☐ Wash windows 017
- ☐ Deep clean window treatments 019
- ☐ Wipe doors and baseboards 023
- ☐ Clean walls 026
- ☐ Clean sconces and light fixtures 067, 070
- ☐ Clean iron 237
- ☐ Clean washer 246, 249, 250
- ☐ Clean dryer vent 254
- ☐ Restock laundry supplies 239, 241
- ☐ Clean lint filter 255

LIVING ROOM

- ☐ Wash windows 017
- ☐ Deep clean window treatments 019
- ☐ Wipe doors and baseboards 023
- ☐ Clean walls 026
- ☐ Clean exterior doors 035
- ☐ Deep clean lampshades 066
- ☐ Clean lamp bases 068
- ☐ Clean light fixtures, chandeliers, and sconces 067, 069, 070
- ☐ Deep clean upholstery 265, 270
- ☐ Deep clean fireplace 281, 282, 283, 284, 285, 286, 287, 288
- ☐ Clean and vacuum bookshelves 293, 294
- ☐ Hire a chimney sweep 281, 284, 285

DINING AREA

- ☐ Wash windows 017
- ☐ Deep clean window treatments 019
- ☐ Wipe doors and baseboards 023
- ☐ Clean walls 026
- ☐ Deep clean lampshades 066
- ☐ Clean lamp bases and sconces 067, 068
- ☐ Clean light fixtures, chandeliers, and sconces 067, 069, 070
- ☐ Polish silver 314
- ☐ Deep clean carpet and pad 303
- ☐ Clean underneath rugs 303
- ☐ Wash floor vents 303

BEDROOM

- ☐ Wash windows 017
- ☐ Deep clean window treatments 019
- ☐ Wipe doors and baseboards 023
- ☐ Deep clean ceilings and walls 026
- ☐ Deep clean lampshades 066
- ☐ Clean lamp bases and sconces 067, 068
- ☐ Clean ceiling fixtures 070
- ☐ Wash pillows and comforters 330, 334
- ☐ Clean mattress 335
- ☐ Treat bed curtains and skirts 337
- ☐ Clean dresser drawers 341
- ☐ Clean ceiling fan 343
- ☐ Clean closet 348
- ☐ Clean and store winter clothing 355

OFFICE

- ☐ Wash windows 017
- ☐ Deep clean window treatments 019
- ☐ Wipe doors and baseboards 023
- ☐ Clean walls 026
- ☐ Deep clean lampshades 066
- ☐ Clean lamp bases and sconces 067, 068
- ☐ Clean fixtures 070
- ☐ Clear computer clutter 363
- ☐ Organize cords 365

CLEANING RECIPES

All the recipes in the chapters throughout this book can be found here for easy reference. Making your own natural cleaning products will not just help the environment, but also save you money that can be better spent on other things.

NOTE: Remember that while natural cleaners can be useful for cleaning and getting that sparkle and shine, they don't quite cut it for sanitizing germy surfaces. For that, turn to an all-purpose cleaner. There are several plant-based disinfectants that are effective at killing bacteria and viruses.

BASIC CLEANERS

ALL-PURPOSE CLEANER
2 tsp. borax
$\frac{1}{4}$ tsp. liquid castile soap
10 drops lemon essential oil

Mix all ingredients with hot water in a 16-oz. spray bottle.

DISINFECTANT
2 tbsp. liquid castile soap
20 drops tea tree oil

Mix the soap and essential oil with hot water in a 16-oz. spray bottle.

GLASS CLEANER
$\frac{1}{4}$ c. distilled white vinegar
5 drops lemon essential oil

Mix all ingredients with hot water in a 16-oz. spray bottle.

NONABRASIVE VINEGAR CLEANER
1 part distilled white vinegar
2 parts water
5 drops essential oil

Combine the vinegar and water in a 16-oz. spray bottle. Add 5 drops of essential oil, such as lavender, grapefruit, orange, lemon, or peppermint, if you don't like the smell of vinegar.

BATHROOM CLEANERS

TOILET BOWL BOMBS
1 $\frac{1}{2}$ c. baking soda
$\frac{1}{2}$ c. citric acid powder
20 drops peppermint essential oil

Thoroughly mix the baking soda and citric acid powder in a bowl. Slowly stir in the peppermint essential oil to evenly distribute. Use a spray bottle to sparingly mist water into the mixture—stirring to uniformly moisten the powder—until the powder sticks together in clumps. The mixture will slightly fizz from the moisture, so make sure not to oversaturate.

Firmly pack a silicone mold with the moist mixture and leave out to dry overnight, wiping off any excess from the fizzing. Gently remove the formed bomb from the mold and store in a sealable container. Add a finished bomb to the toilet bowl and allow to fizz. Once the bomb has dissolved, flush out the bowl water.

TOILET BOWL CLEANER
Liquid castile soap
$\frac{1}{2}$ c. baking soda

Squirt the liquid castile soap under the rim of the toilet bowl, then sprinkle the baking soda into the bowl. Scrub with a toilet brush, and flush to rinse.

GROUT CLEANER
$\frac{3}{4}$ c. baking soda
$\frac{1}{2}$ c. hydrogen peroxide
2–3 c. water

Mix all ingredients into a paste, apply to the grout, and let sit for 15 minutes. Scrub with a grout brush or toothbrush, staying within the grout lines.

TUB 'N' TILE CLEANER
$\frac{1}{2}$ c. borax
$\frac{1}{2}$ c. baking soda
1 tsp. liquid castile soap
2–3 c. hot water

Thoroughly mix all ingredients in a bucket.

CARPET AND FURNITURE CLEANERS

BASIC CARPET STAIN REMOVER

$\frac{1}{4}$ tsp. castile soap

Mix soap with water in a 16-oz. spray bottle.

FURNITURE POLISH

$\frac{1}{2}$ c. jojoba oil

2 tbsp. distilled white vinegar

5 drops lemon essential oil

Pour all ingredients in a sealable 8-oz. jar. Vigorously shake to emulsify before using.

VINEGAR-BASED CARPET STAIN REMOVER

1 tbsp. castile soap

1 tbsp. white vinegar

2 c. warm water

Mix all ingredients in a 16-oz. spray bottle.

FLOOR CLEANERS

ALL-PURPOSE FLOOR CLEANER

1 tsp. almond castile soap

$^1/_4$ c. distilled white vinegar

10 drops orange essential oil

10 drops clove essential oil

Mix all ingredients with hot water in a 24-oz. spray bottle.

LAMINATE FLOOR CLEANER

$^3/_4$ c. distilled white vinegar

$^3/_4$ c. rubbing alcohol

10 drops peppermint essential oil

$^3/_4$ c. hot water

Mix all ingredients in a 24-oz. spray bottle. Use sparingly to minimize the chance of warping.

HARDWOOD FLOOR CLEANER

1 tsp. almond castile soap

10 drops lemon essential oil

Mix all ingredients with hot water in a 24-oz. spray bottle. Use sparingly to minimize the chance of warping; do not use on unsealed hardwoods.

TILE FLOOR CLEANER

$^1/_4$ c. distilled white vinegar

15 drops orange essential oil

Mix all ingredients with hot water in a 24-oz. spray bottle.

VINYL FLOOR CLEANER

$^1/_4$ c. distilled white vinegar

3 tbsp. borax

10 drops lemon essential oil

10 drops lavender essential oil

Mix all ingredients with hot water in a 24-oz. spray bottle.

KITCHEN CLEANERS

GARBAGE DISPOSAL BOMBS
Makes 24 bombs.

$^1/_2$ c. citric acid

1 $^1/_2$ c. baking soda

30 drops orange essential oil

Mix all ingredients in a bowl until thoroughly combined. Use a spray bottle to mist just enough water for the mixture to hold its shape. Mold the mixture into small balls with a rounded tablespoon and place on a cookie sheet to dry overnight. Store in an airtight container.

DRAIN CLEANER
1 c. table salt

1 c. baking soda

2–3 qt. water

1 c. distilled vinegar

Thoroughly mix the salt and baking soda in a small bowl. Boil the water in a kettle. Pour the salt and baking soda mixture down the drain, then slowly pour the vinegar into the drain. Let it bubble for 1 to 2 minutes. Clear the drain by pouring in the boiling water. Wipe the drain cover with a soft cloth to make sure no salt or vinegar remains.

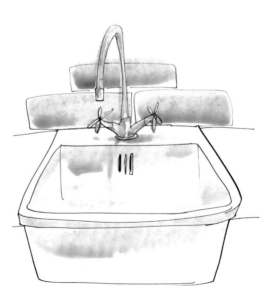

LAUNDRY CLEANERS

BLEACHING SOLUTION

1 c. hydrogen peroxide

$^1/_4$ c. lemon juice

3 qt. water

Thoroughly mix all ingredients in a large container. Pour 1 to 2 c. per wash load into the bleach dispenser.

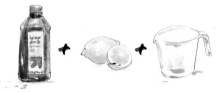

LAUNDRY STRIPPER

$^1/_4$ c. borax

$^1/_4$ c. washing soda

$^1/_2$ c. powdered laundry detergent

Fill your bathtub with hot water and add all ingredients, stir until they're dissolved, then add the washed and dried clothes or linens. Swish the mixture around every hour for 4 to 6 hours, then drain the bathtub and wash the laundry in a regular cycle in your washing machine (no detergent needed).

LAVENDER ROOM SPRAY

1 $^1/_2$ oz. rubbing alcohol

1 $^1/_2$ oz. water

30 drops lavender essential oil

Mix all ingredients in a 4-oz. spray bottle. Shake well before each use.

INDEX

weldon**owen**

an imprint of Insight Editions
P.O. Box 3088
San Rafael, CA 94912
www.weldonowen.com

Follow us on Facebook:
www.facebook.com/weldonowen/

Follow us on Twitter:
@WeldonOwen

Follow us on Instagram:
weldonowen

CEO Raoul Goff
VP Publisher Roger Shaw
Editorial Director Katie Killebrew
VP Creative Chrissy Kwasnik
VP Manufacturing Alix Nicholaeff
Art Director Allister Fein
Designer Jean Hwang
Senior Editor John Foster
Production Manager Sam Taylor

Weldon Owen would like to thank Catie Parrish,
Bob Cooper, Diedre Hammons, and Kevin Broccoli.

ISBN: 978-1-68188-837-8

Printed in China

First printed in 2022

2025 2024 2023 2022 ● 10 9 8 7 6 5 4 3 2 1

CREDITS

Illustrations by Louise Morgan
© Weldon Owen International

Photographs with tips 014, 042, 076, 170,
and 267 by Aubrie Pick
© Weldon Owen International

Unless otherwise noted above, all
photography © Shutterstock